Mrs Dolby's
MEMORY
MAGIC

Karen Dolby has written twelve books, but finds
it hard to remember their titles. She has two
children for whom she has to remember
everything, and a husband who finds it hard
to remember what day of the week it is.
She wrote this book for him.

Mrs Dolby's

MEMORY MAGIC

*A Compendium of Tools, Tips and
Exercises to Help You Remember Everything*

Karen Dolby

arrow books

This paperback edition published by Arrow Books 2010

10 9 8 7 6 5 4 3 2 1

Copyright © Karen Dolby, 2009, 2010

First published in Great Britain in 2009 by Preface Publishing
20 Vauxhall Bridge Road
London SW1V 2SA

An imprint of The Random House Group Limited

www.rbooks.co.uk

Addresses for companies within The Random House Group Limited
can be found at www.randomhouse.co.uk

The Random House Group Limited Reg. No. 954009

A CIP catalogue record for this book is available from the British Library

ISBN 978 1 84809 248 8

The Random House Group Limited supports the Forest Stewardship
Council (FSC), the leading international forest certification organisation.
All our titles that are printed on Greenpeace-approved FSC-certified paper
carry the FSC logo. Our paper procurement policy can be found at
www.rbooks.co.uk/environment

Mixed Sources
Product group from well-managed
forests and other controlled sources
www.fsc.org   Cert no. TT-COC-2139
© 1996 Forest Stewardship Council

Designed and typeset in Filosofia by Peter Ward
Printed and bound in Great Britain by CPI Bookmarque, Croydon CRO 4TD

For Trevor, George and Freya

CONTENTS

INTRODUCTION

> *'Study without desire spoils the memory, and it retains nothing that it takes in.'*

LEONARDO DA VINCI

How often have you heard the complaints 'I've got a terrible memory,' 'My brain's like a sieve,' or 'I simply forget everything'? At some point in our busy lives, most of us wish we had a better memory. But it's not that you have a bad memory, it's simply that you are not using it efficiently.

From the moment we are born, and perhaps even before that, our brain takes in information which it processes, encodes and then stores away. When people complain they have a bad memory what they are really saying is that they have trouble retrieving their memories – all the facts and information are safely locked in the brain, the problem is access. It's easy to upgrade the memory on a computer – just find a compatible system. What most people don't realise is that it's just as simple to do the same for your brain. All it takes is a little know-how and training.

Winston Churchill famously made a point of never memorising his speeches verbatim after one disastrous occasion when his mind went completely blank. What he did instead was to memorise what he wanted to say, the key points, along with a few suitably elegant, clever or stirring phrases. Daniel Tammet, who won worldwide acclaim for his memoir of life with autistic savant syndrome, believes that the differences between savant and non-savant minds are exaggerated and that his astonishing feats of memory are the result of complex associative ways of thinking which we can all aspire to.

Many of the greatest actors, linguists and speech-makers don't have naturally brilliant memories: what they do have at their fingertips is a range of memory systems and mnemonic tools to help them. You simply need to find the techniques and tricks that work for you.

Mnemonics help your memory function more efficiently by using a number of different devices including rhymes, sentences, diagrams, acronyms and rules to easily retrieve names, dates, lists, facts and figures. The word comes from the Greek *mneme* meaning memory and *mnemon* meaning mindful, and Mnemosyne was the ancient Greek goddess of memory, mother of the Muses.

Mnemonics work because they force your mind to really pay attention to what you're learning. So often we instantly forget someone's name when first introduced simply because we didn't listen properly, our mind already thinking of our next comment. Mnemonics also help to organise the information, which again makes it easier to retrieve later. Research shows that mental capacity to remember can be vastly increased by simply breaking numbers or letters into groups. This breakdown is usually called chunking and works particularly well if the chunks can be made memorable. The ideal length for chunking letters and numbers is three, which explains the way in which most telephone numbers are broken up.

Many mnemonics are so much a part of everyday use we often don't realise we are using a memory device. For instance 'Spring forward, fall back' reminds us the clocks go forward one hour in spring and back in autumn, or the rhyme we all learn in school to remember the number of days in each month:

> 30 days hath September,
> April, June and November,
> All the rest have 31,
> Except February alone,
> Which has 28 days clear,
> And 29 in each leap year.

It's interesting that most people have no difficulty reciting this absolutely correctly as other 31-day months could easily be substituted for the four 30-day months and the rhyme would still work.

In this book I will be reminding you of all the mnemonics you've ever learned and possibly forgotten, along with plenty of new ones. There are also clear explanations of the different memory systems used by memory masters. I have tried to be as comprehensive and wide-ranging as possible but the topics covered are a subjective list. They are all areas that I remember from childhood and others that have interested me since. Sometimes several mnemonics are suggested for the same thing. This is because different ideas appeal to different people and for a mnemonic to work well it has to mean something: whether it is funny or just appeals, there needs to be a connection, it has to spark an image and emotional response in order to be memorable.

One of the most important things I have learned while researching this book is that for most people there is no such thing as a good or bad memory. Putting aside all the clever memory systems and thousands of punchy mnemonics, the key is really effort and interest. People with so-called 'good' memories usually work at it, they practise and take time to learn and improve. But while there are no instant short cuts, this does mean that a better memory is a real possibility for everyone.

And there are definite benefits. There's a growing body of evidence suggesting that mental training in a subject that interests you improves not only memory but cognitive functioning. To quote the director of the Memory Clinic at Johns Hopkins, Barry Gordon, 'If you want to improve your mental functioning, pick something you are interested in and work at it.'

'Nothing fixes a thing so intensely in the memory as the wish to forget it.'

MICHEL DE MONTAIGNE

Mrs Dolby's

MEMORY MAGIC

A Compendium of Tools, Tips and
Exercises to Help You Remember Everything

THE LINK AND STORY METHOD –
REMEMBERING A SIMPLE LIST

The Link method is probably one of the most basic mnemonic techniques. It is easy to understand and worth mastering before moving on to some of the other memory techniques. At its most simple it works by linking words together using images but before I explain it fully take a moment to test yourself. Study the following list of random words – really take the time to try to remember them, then turn the book over and write down the words in order.

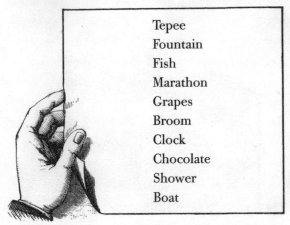

Tepee
Fountain
Fish
Marathon
Grapes
Broom
Clock
Chocolate
Shower
Boat

How far did you get? And if asked to write the same list backwards or in ten minutes' time how many words would you remember then? But if you assign each word an image and then link it to the next you will find with a little practice you can do much better.

The key to mastering this technique is to make each image as vivid and unusual as possible. Each should interact or link with the next, it won't work simply to imagine one standing beside the next. For instance, the fountain should actually be erupting from the top of the tepee, which instead of fabric could be carved from stone with strange carvings on the sides.

The important thing is that the image should mean something to you. It could be personal or just something that amuses or even disgusts you. Laughter is always helpful for keeping something in mind and likewise repellent ideas are hard to forget.

So bearing all this in mind, the pictures for the list could go something like this:

A carved stone Tepee erupts into a Fountain that is flowing with giant Fish with gnashing teeth. When they hit the ground the Fish grow legs and run a Marathon, snapping at the heels of the other runners. The other runners appear to be Grapes, purple, bloated and overripe, oozing pus-like juice. A giant cartoon Broom appears from the sky and sweeps the Grapes away. The Broom has a long handle and swings rhythmically to and fro as it is the pendulum of a huge sun Clock. The Clock darkens as it is made of Chocolate melting in the heat, the numbers and hands lengthening and distorting as it begins to drip. The Chocolate drips are now gushing from a Shower, which is attached to a bathtub Boat bobbing up and down; inside a rower bails frantically as chocolate cascades from the Shower filling his bath Boat.

Read this carefully, picturing each cameo as you go, then turn the book over and try writing out the list again. Let each image lead you effortlessly on to the next. It's surprising how much easier it is to remember everything.

This was only a very short list, but try this technique next time you go shopping. By linking each item on your list with an entertaining image, you'll find yourself becoming ever more ingenious and you can develop the Link method further by weaving a story around your pictures. Be creative and let your imagination run wild and don't be afraid to add sound effects or vibrant colours if these work well for you.

The Link method is not only useful for remembering lists, you can also use it to remind yourself to do something. For instance if you promised to ring a friend before supper, imagine their face on the cooker smiling up at you, mouthing the words 'Call me', or picture them as the wooden spoon you use to stir your soup.

Even speeches can be learned by representing each of the points you need to make by clear images, vividly linked together. Once you are practised in the technique, you will be able to do away with notes altogether and appear far more relaxed and confident. In the same way you can learn poems or your part in a play or apply the method to help with revision for exams recalling events, theories or case studies.

WHERE MEMORIES ARE STORED IN THE BRAIN

The hippocampus is one of the main parts of the brain involved in the forming, sorting and storing of memories. Not only does the hippocampus store memories but it also connects them with other related memories giving meaning and context.

The hippocampus is located in the medial temporal lobe of the brain. Early scientists likened the shape to a ram's horn or seahorse and the sixteenth-century anatomist Julius Caesar Arazi gave the structure its Greek name meaning 'sea horse'. Together with the adjacent amygdala, the hippocampus forms the central axis of the limbic system, the emotion system of the brain, in charge of the transfer of information into memory.

LANGUAGE

'Memory feeds imagination.'
AMY TAN

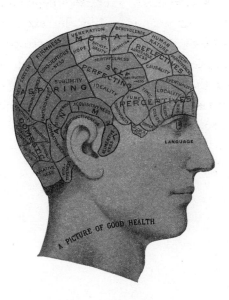

A PICTURE OF GOOD HEALTH

The first mnemonics I ever learned are all connected with learning to read and write, and I suspect I am not unusual in this. In fact so ingrained in my memory are these simple rhymes, chants and catchphrases that I don't even remember being taught them. They simply spring to mind automatically, particularly for spellings.

SPELLING BEE

One of the many peculiarities of the English language is the rules on spelling which always apply, except when they don't. There are several rhyming phrases taught to schoolchildren from time immemorial to help them recall certain of these rules.

Perhaps the most common is:
   'I' before 'E' except after 'C'.

Although sadly this rule does not always apply, which has led to:
   'I' before 'E' except after 'C'
   Though 'weird' is just 'weird'.

(And so incidentally are Budweiser, feisty, forfeit, heifer, height, heirloom, kaleidoscope, leisure, seismic, seize and weir, to list but a few.)

The other main exceptions to the rule are words where 'EI' is pronounced as 'A', for instance, abseil, reign and feign, which have prompted this version:

'I' before 'E' except after 'C'
Or when sounded like 'A' as in neighbour and weigh.

CATCHPHRASES/WORDPLAY

Clever or rhythmic phrases can also help with spelling:
To spell **cemetery** with three e's, remember:
She cried, 'E . . . e . . . e!' as she ran past the cemetery.

Friend or freind?
You always need friends to the end.

Argument or arguement?
Argue lost an 'e' in an argument.

To recall the number of 'Cs' in **necessary** and **success**:
Only one 'C' is necessary but you need two 'Cs' for success.

There are various chants that work for **Mississippi**:
· *Say to yourself, 'M-I-S, S-I-S, S-I-P, P-I'. Try it out loud; there is a natural rhythm which begins to make sense the more you say it.*
· *Or you may prefer 'Mrs M, Mrs I, Mrs S S I, Mrs S S I, Mrs P P I.'*

In a similar vein, Roald Dahl spelt out **difficulty** in *Matilda*:
'Mrs D, Mrs I, Mrs F F I, Mrs C, Mrs U, Mrs L T Y.'

To spell **separate**, use this story:
There was once a farmer named Sep and when his wife saw a rat she yelled, 'Sep, a rat! E!!!'

There are two options for **together**:
We went to get her.
Or you may prefer:
Remember if you get her you'll be together.

Ascertain
When you ascertain a fact, always be As Certain as you possibly can.

Bookkeeper
Triple compound: oo kk ee.

Potassium
Remember one tea but two sugars.

Slaughter (which always makes me smile)
Slaughter is simply Laughter with an S at the beginning.

Innocent
IN No CENTury is murder an innocent crime.

SPELLING ACRONYMS

Take the initial letter of each word in a memorable sentence to correctly spell words which people often find tricky.

Mnemonics
Mnemonics Now Erase Man's Oldest Nemesis: Insufficient Cerebral Storage.

Necessary
Never Eat Crisps, Eat Salad Sandwiches And Remain Young.

Rhythm
Rhythm Has Your Two Hips Moving.

Because
Big Elephants Can Always Understand Small Elephants.

Arithmetic
A Rat In The House Might Eat The Ice Cream.

Wednesday
WE Do Not Eat Soup DAY, or more simply and certainly the way I always think of the word, just sound out Wed-nes-day.

Geography
General Eisenhower's Old Grandfather Rode A Pig Home Yesterday.

Ocean
Only Cats' Eyes Are Narrow.

COMMON CONFUSIONS

Homophones are words which sound the same (or similar) but have different spellings and meanings.

Affect the effect
The word 'raven' can help you remember when to use 'affect' and when 'effect' is the correct choice.

R *emember*
A *ffect*
V *erb*
E *ffect*
N *oun*

Desert desserts
Remember a desert is sandy with only one 'S', while desserts have two 'Ss' like sweet stuff, strawberry shortcake and two scoops of ice cream. If you eat too many desserts you may feel stressed which helpfully is simply desserts spelled backwards.

Hear, here
You hear with your ear.

Stationary stationery
To be sure of the difference, remember that:
A station stAnds still – it's stationAry, and
A stationEr sElls stationEry.

Sculpture and sculptor
> *A sculptor works with stone to create a sculPTURE which is a kind of PicTURE.*

The principles of principals
> *Your princiPAL is your PAL (in a perfect world), while the ruLEs he lives by can be called principLEs and both end in LE.*

There and They're
> *There is a place just like here.*
> *They're is when they want to say they are.*

COORDINATING CONJUNCTIONS

BOAF SYN

Is an acronym for:
> But
> Or
> And
> For
> So
> Yet
> Nor

ONOMATOPOEIA

A strange-looking word which comes from two Greek words meaning 'name' and 'I make'. An onomatopoeia sounds like the thing it is describing, for instance, buzz, squelch, cuckoo (which hasn't changed from its Anglo-Saxon origins), ping-pong, swish and cartoon expletives such as thwack, wham, biff and pow.

Onomatopoeias are sometimes called literary mnemonics and are popular devices in advertising because they automatically remind you of exactly what they are describing: just think of the slogan 'Snap, crackle and pop' for Rice Krispies or 'Clunk, click every trip' in the campaign started in the 70s prompting everyone to fasten their seat belts.

There are onomatopoeias in every language from 'tuxtux' which is the Latin equivalent of bam or whack, to 'dodidoki' to describe a heart beating in Japanese. They are also used as mnemonics in music, for example in kuchi shoga, the Japanese system for pronouncing drum sounds.

To remember how to correctly spell onomatopoeia, sound out the first part: On O Mato then use the acronym 'Points Of Exaggeration In Art' for the last bit.

FIGURES OF SPEECH

Most People Sing In Harmony usefully recalls:
Metaphor, Personification, Simile, Irony, Hyperbole.

SPLIT INFINITIVES

This describes a sentence where an adverb is placed between the infinitive marker 'to' and the verb itself. Perhaps the easiest way to remember is simply to recall possibly the most famous example of all time from the opening sequence of *Star Trek*:

'**To boldly go** where no man has gone before.'

Although traditional grammar views splitting the infinitive as incorrect, particularly in formal, written English, the rule is gradually disappearing. Many writers feel that the most natural position for the adverb is often between 'to' and the verb, for example: 'George promised to really try this time'; and that avoiding the split simply results in clumsier sentences.

PALINDROMES

A palindrome is a word or phrase which reads the same forwards and backwards, for example, the name Anna, and words such as deified and reviver. Numbers and sequences can also be palindromes.

The discovery of graffiti at Herculaneum depicting a palindromic word square shows that palindromes date back to at least the first century when Herculaneum was engulfed by a pyroclastic mudflow following the eruption of Vesuvius in AD79.

S	A	T	O	R
A	R	E	P	O
T	E	N	E	T
O	P	E	R	A
R	O	T	A	S

The word 'arepo' is unknown to translators, which makes the meaning debateable. It is sometimes translated as, 'The sower Arepo holds the wheels at work' but it may also have been a secret Christian sign with 'Tenet' (from *tenere* meaning to hold) forming a cross.

USEFUL TERMS TO REMEMBER/ LANGUAGE AND GRAMMAR

Every name is called a Noun
Like field and fountain, street and town.

In place of a noun the Pronoun stands
For he, she and it can clap their hands.

An Adjective describes a thing
Like magic wand and feathered wing.

The Verb means action something done
To read, to write, to walk, to run.

How things are done, the Adverbs tell
Like quickly, slowly, badly, well.

A Preposition shows relation
Like in the street, or at the station.

Conjunctions join in different ways
Sentences, words or thought and phrase.

An Interjection suggests surprise
As Oh! How splendid! Oh my! You're wise!

Through poetry we learn how each
Makes up the different parts of speech.

Prefixes

A prefix is a small group of letters, which often come from Greek or Latin, which are added to the beginning of a word to alter its meaning: for example, **dis**appear, **mis**inform; **extra**ordinary.

Suffixes

Suffixes are also added to words to change their function or meaning but are attached to the end rather than the beginning. For example '-ly' turns an adjective into an adverb: the adjectives 'wild' and 'careful' become the adverbs 'wildly' and 'carefully'; or the addition of 'man' to 'work' (workman) or 'wright' to 'play' to create 'playwright'.

To remember the difference between the two, just think of the word previous for prefix or simply that 'p' comes before 's' in the alphabet.

ELEMENTS OF STORIES

Very Many Pupils Come To School.
    Reminds us to include: Viewpoint, Mood, Plot, Characters, Theme, Setting.

LITERARY GENRES

Just remember '3Ps'
    Plays, Poetry, Prose.

Practise the Link and Story Method (page 3), or one of the other memory systems described later, to learn this simple list of words.

THE TEN MOST COMMONLY USED WORDS IN THE ENGLISH LANGUAGE

There are various definitive lists, all different. The following list was compiled by Oxford Online in association with the

Oxford English Dictionary – which seems a reliable source to consult.

1	the	6	a
2	be	7	in
3	to	8	that
4	of	9	have
5	and	10	I

LITERATURE

'If any one faculty of our nature may be called more wonderful than the rest, I do think it is memory. There seems something more speakingly incomprehensible in the powers, the failures, the inequalities of memory, than in any other of our intelligences. The memory is sometimes so retentive, so serviceable, so obedient; at others, so bewildered and so weak; and at others again, so tyrannic, so beyond control! We are, to be sure, a miracle every way; but our powers of recollecting and of forgetting do seem peculiarly past finding out.'

JANE AUSTEN,
Mansfield Park

JANE AUSTEN

(16 December 1775 – 18 July 1817)

Jane Austen is one of the most famous and beloved of English novelists. Her books provide a wonderful insight into the lives of the middle and upper classes, particularly women, in the early 19th century. Renowned for her wit and social observation, her novels were originally published anonymously, simply stating they were by 'A Lady'. Since 1833 when they were first published in a collected edition, they have never been out of print. Though she was little known during her short lifetime, Jane's nephew, James Edward Austen-Leigh, published *A Memoir of Jane Austen* in 1869 which introduced her to a wider audience and rekindled interest. From that time her worldwide fan base of Janeites has grown steadily, reflected in numerous films and TV adaptations of her life and works.

How to remember her published novels

Sense and Sensibility, 1811
Pride and Prejudice, 1813
Mansfield Park, 1814
Emma, 1816

Northanger Abbey }
Persuasion } published posthumously in 1818

a Sense of Pride Makes Emma Notably Perky.

Or you may prefer:

Senseless Pride Makes Everyone Notoriously Prickly.

As well as her novels, Jane Austen wrote three unfinished works of fiction: *Lady Susan*, 1794 and 1805; *The Watsons*, 1804; and *Sanditon*, 1817. She also wrote three volumes of juvenilia begun while still in her teens; *Sir Charles Grandison*, 1793 and 1800; *Plan of a Novel*, 1815; poems and prayers. Of an estimated 3000 letters, only about 160 survive. After her death, Jane's sister Cassandra burnt many and censored others. More were later destroyed by the family of her brother, Admiral Francis Austen.

WILLIAM SHAKESPEARE
(23 April 1564 – 23 April 1616)

It's one thing to devise a simple mnemonic acronym for the novels of Jane Austen, but what if you want to remember everything that Shakespeare ever wrote?

One option is to apply one of the memory systems; for instance the Link system might help if you can visualise an image for each play (there are 37 in case you're wondering, or 38 if you accept *The Two Noble Kinsmen*; and then of course there are the sonnets and poems). Star-crossed lovers obviously for *Romeo and Juliet*; spirits, a magician and monstrous creature whirling above a storm-lashed sea in *The Tempest*; Shakespeare's caricature of a hunchbacked loathsome king in *Richard III* and so on. You don't have to know the play to think of an image, just let the wording of the title suggest something you will find memorable however unconnected with Shakespeare.

It also helps to break down the lists as much as possible and alphabetising also always helps me to order things in my mind.

And so we have:

Comedies

All's Well That Ends Well
As You Like It
The Comedy of Errors
Love's Labours Lost
Measure for Measure
The Merry Wives of Windsor
The Merchant of Venice
A Midsummer Night's Dream
Much Ado About Nothing
Pericles, Prince of Tyre
Taming of the Shrew
The Tempest
Twelfth Night
Two Gentlemen of Verona
The Two Noble Kinsmen (attributed to Shakespeare
    and John Fletcher)
A Winter's Tale

Histories

Henry IV, Part 1
Henry IV, Part 2
Henry V
Henry VI, Part 1
Henry VI, Part 2
Henry VI, Part 3
Henry VIII
King John
Richard II
Richard III

Tragedies

Antony and Cleopatra
Coriolanus
Cymbeline
Hamlet
Julius Caesar
King Lear
Macbeth
Othello
Romeo and Juliet
Timon of Athens
Titus Andronicus
Troilus and Cressida
(*Cymbeline* and *Troilus and Cressida* are sometimes labelled 'problem plays' by critics and not always regarded as tragedies as they do not conform strictly to the rules of

tragedy. Partly for this reason, sometimes a fourth category of plays labelled romance is introduced.)

Poetry

Sonnets
A Lover's Complaint
The Rape of Lucrece
Venus and Adonis
Funeral Elegy

MEMORISING

When trying to fix anything in your memory it is always useful to try to write it down from memory and then compare with the original. After you have checked and made any corrections, try again after an hour, then a day, a week and at regular intervals.

Shakespeare's life

William Shakespeare is regarded by many as the greatest playwright of all time yet very little is known for certain of his life. We know he was born in Stratford-upon-Avon in 1564 and died, aged 52, in 1616 on his birthday, 23 April (also rather appropriately for such a notable Englishman, St George's Day). He married Anne Hathaway in 1582 at the age of 18 and they had three children, Susanna and the twins, Hamnet and

Judith. At some point between 1585 and 1592 he moved to London without his family to forge his career as an actor and writer. He was a prominent member of the theatre company the Chamberlain's Men, later called the King's Men, which built and occupied the Globe Theatre on the river Thames from 1599. Over the course of his career, Shakespeare became the most popular playwright in England and was patronised by both Queen Elizabeth I and King James I.

Although also celebrated for his Sonnets, 'the play's the thing!' (Hamlet, Act 2, scene 2) and rarely a minute goes past without one of his plays being performed somewhere in the world, whether on a school or a professional stage.

LINES TO REMEMBER

There is nothing quite so satisfying for testing your memory as knowing a few poems or lines of Shakespeare by heart. Once learned they tend to stick. There are lines and quotations I learned at school which I mentally revisit on occasions almost to check they are still there and to reassure me my memory is still working. They are also useful as party tricks, in times of boredom or stress, and even to recite aloud in the darkness while trying to coax a determinedly wide awake small child to sleep. I found I could choose the lines; the important thing was that they flowed mellifluously and encouraged afore-mentioned insomniac to drift sweetly to sleep 'perchance to dream'.

The choice of passage should be your own. Choose something you like, for whatever reason. It should be a passage you find memorable or which speaks to you. These are among my favourites.

Jacques' speech on the Seven Ages of Man:

'All the world's a stage,
And all the men and women merely players:
They have their exits and their entrances;
And one man in his time plays many parts,
His acts being seven ages. At first the infant,
Mewling and puking in the nurse's arms.
And then the whining school-boy, with his satchel,
And shining morning face, creeping like snail
Unwillingly to school. And then the lover,
Sighing like furnace, with a woeful ballad
Made to his mistress' eyebrow. Then a soldier,
Full of strange oaths, and bearded like the pard,
Jealous in honour, sudden and quick in quarrel,
Seeking the bubble reputation
Even in the cannon's mouth. And then the justice,
In fair round belly with good capon lined,
With eyes severe, and beard of formal cut,
Full of wise saws and modern instances;
And so he plays his part. The sixth age shifts
Into the lean and slipper'd pantaloon,
With spectacles on nose and pouch on side,
His youthful hose well saved, a world too wide
For his shrunk shank; and his big manly voice,

Turning again toward childish treble, pipes
And whistles in his sound. Last scene of all,
That ends this strange eventful history,
Is second childishness and mere oblivion,
Sans teeth, sans eyes, sans taste, sans every thing.'

As You Like It, Act II, scene VII, *c.* 1599

Hamlet's famous musings on the futility of life and mortality, quoted to poignant effect by Richard E. Grant in the final scene of the film *Withnail and I*:

'I have of late, but wherefore I know not, lost all my
mirth, foregone all custom of exercises; and indeed it
goes so heavily with my disposition that this goodly
frame, the earth, seems to me a sterile promontory;
this most excellent canopy, the air, look you, this brave
o'erhanging firmament, this majestical roof fretted
with golden fire, why, it appears no other thing to me
than a foul and pestilent congregation of vapours.
What a piece of work is a man! how noble in reason!
how infinite in faculty! in form and moving how
express and admirable! in action how like an angel! in
apprehension how like a god! the beauty of the world!
the paragon of animals! And yet, to me, what is this
quintessence of dust? Man delights not me; no, nor
women neither . . .'

Hamlet, Act II, scene II, *c.* 1600

And Enobarbus says of 'that lass unparalled', Cleopatra:

> 'Age cannot wither her, nor custom stale
> Her infinite variety; other women cloy
> The appetites they feed, but she makes hungry
> Where most she satisfies . . .'
>
> *Antony and Cleopatra*, Act II, scene II, *c.* 1607

&ec HOW &ec
TO LEARN A FOREIGN
LANGUAGE

'Grasp the subject, the words will follow.'

Cato the Elder

In *Use Your Memory*, Tony Buzan explains that a mere one hundred words make up about fifty per cent of the total number of words used in an average conversation. It follows that by learning this basic one hundred you will vastly improve your ability to speak another language. Obviously you would also need to check extra vocabulary but learning one hundred foreign words seems an easily achievable target for most people.

As with the 'ten most common words in English' (see page 19) there is some dispute about exactly which words are the most commonly used in French, but Buzan suggests these as the basic one hundred:

1. A	5. Almost	9. Because
Un/une	*Presque*	*Parce que*
2. After	6. Also	10. Before
Après	*Aussi*	*Avant*
3. Again	7. Always	11. Big
Encore	*Toujours*	*Grand*
4. All	8. And	12. But
Chacun des	*Et*	*Mais*

13. I can
Je peux

14. I come
Je viens

15. Either/or
L'un ou l'autre

16. I find
Je trouve

17. First
Premiers

18. For
Pour

19. Friend
L'ami

20. From
De

21. I go
Je vais

22. Good
Bon

23. Goodbye
Au revoir

24. Happy
Heureux

25. I have
J'ai

26. He
Il

27. Hello
Bonjour

28. Here
Ici

29. How
Comment

30. I
Je

31. I am
Je suis

32. If
Si

33. In
Dans

34. I know
Je sais

35. Last
Dernier

36. I like
J'aime

37. Little
Petit

38. Love
L'amour

39. I make
Je fais

40. Many
Beaucoup de

41. One
Un/une

42. More
Plus

43. Most
La plupart de

44. Much
Beaucoup

45. My
Mon, ma, mes

46. New
Nouveau

47. No
Non

48. Not
Pas

49. Now
Maintenant

50. Of
De

51. Often
Souvent

52. On
Sur

53. I would like
Je voudrais

54. Only
Seulement

55. Or
Ou

56. Other
Autre

57. Our
Notre/nos

58. Out
Dehors

59. Over
Plus de

60. People
Les gens

61. Place
L'endroit

62. Please
S'il vous plaît

63. The same
Le même

64. I see
Je vois

65. She
Elle

66. So
Alors
(So much)
Tellement

67. Some
Quelques

68. Sometimes
Quelquefois

69. Still
Encore

70. Such
Si
(Such and such)
Tel, telle

71. I tell/say
Je dis

72. Thank you
Merci

73. That
Ce, cet, cette

74. The
Le, la, les

75. Their
Leur, leurs

76. Them
Ils, Elles

77. Then
Puis

78. There is
Il y a

79. They
Ils

80. Thing
La chose

81. I think
Je pense

82. This
Ce, cet, cette

83. Time
Temps

84. To
À

85. Under
Sous

86. Up here
Ici

Up there
Là-haut

87. Us
Nous

88. To use
Utiliser

89. Very
Très

90. We
Nous

91. What?
Comment

92. When
Quand

93. Where
Où

94. Which
Quel

95. Who
Qui

96. Why
Pourquoi

97. With
Avec

98. Yes
Oui

99. You
Vous, tu

100. Your
Votre, Vos

© *Use Your Memory*, Tony Buzan, BBC Worldwide Limited

Past Tense

One of the most useful acronyms for anyone learning French is:

DR and *MRS VAN DER TRAMP*

to remember the 16 verbs which take 'etre' in the Past or Perfect tense.

They are:

Verb	*Meaning*	*Past participle*
devenir	to become	devenu
revenir	to come back	revenu
monter	to go up	monté
rester	to stay	resté
sortir	to go out	sorti
venir	to come	venu
aller	to go	allé
naître	to be born	né
descendre	to go down	descendu
entrer	to enter	entré
retourner	to return (somewhere)	retourné
tomber	to fall	tombé
rentrer	to return home	rentré
arriver	to arrive	arrivé
mourir	to die	mort
partir	to leave	parti

ROMANCE LANGUAGES

To recall which are classified as Romance languages, simply think of:

FRIPS

French, Romanian, Italian, Portugese, Spanish.

GENERAL KNOWLEDGE

*'Own only what you can carry with you;
know language, know countries, know people.
Let your memory be your travel bag.'*

ALEXANDER SOLZHENITSYN

This section could as easily have been called 'Miscellaneous', or I could have tried to fit each of the topics into more specific sections. However, they seemed to work as a random group of subjects which you may or may not come across or wonder about at some point in everyday life.

BURNING FIREWOOD

My mother-in-law, the most skilled hearth fire maker I know, first made me aware that when it comes to firewood, not all woods are equal. She remembered some but not quite all of this ancient rhyme to guide you in your choice of suitable timber to warm your home:

> Beech log fires burn bright and clear,
> Though only if they're kept a year;
> Store your beech for Christmastide,
> With fresh-cut holly laid beside.
> Chestnut's only good, they say,
> If for years 'tis stored away.
> Birch and fir wood burn too fast,
> Blaze too bright and do not last.

Flames from larch will flicker up high,
Dangerously the sparks will fly.
But ash wood green and ash wood brown
Are fit for a queen with a golden crown.

Oaken logs, if dry and old,
Keep away the winter's cold.
Poplar gives a bitter smoke,
Stings your eyes and makes you choke.
Elm wood burns like churchyard mould,
Even the very flames are cold.
Hawthorn bakes the sweetest bread,
So in Ireland it is said.
Apple wood will scent a room,
Pear wood smells like flowers in bloom.
But ash wood wet and ash wood dry
A king may warm his slippers by.

TEMPERATURES IN CELSIUS

30 is hot, 20 is nice, 10 is cold, zero is ice.

CHAMPAGNE BOTTLE SIZES

The smaller ones are easy to remember: there is the usual quarter bottle, half-bottle and bottle, but what comes next?

	Number of standard bottles	
Magnum	2 bottles	1.5 litres
Jeroboam	4 bottles	3 litres
Rehoboam	6 bottles	4.5 litres
Methuselah	8 bottles	6 litres
Salmanazar	12 bottles	9 litres
Balthazar	16 bottles	12 litres
Nebuchadnezzar	20 bottles	15 litres
Melchior	24 bottles	18 litres

The largest of these have a celebratory value but are hardly practical: a Nebuchadnezar weighs a staggering 38 kilos and there is some question of quality as pressure can be lost. There are also a few additional sizes occasionally made to mark special occasions or for particular customers. One notable example are the Imperial pint-sized bottles which Pol Roger made for Sir Winston Churchill, brought to him promptly each morning at 11.

All of these bottles are named after biblical, usually Old Testament, figures, with the exception of Magnum, which is alternatively an ice cream or an 80s TV series starring Tom Selleck.

Jeroboam was the founder and first king of Israel; Rehoboam was the son of King Solomon and ruler of Judah;

Methuselah was Noah's grandfather, famed for living to the very grand old age of 969 and dying in the year of the Great Flood; Salmanazar (or Salmaneser) I, II, III, IV and V were all kings of Assyria; Balthazar was regent of Babylon and also commonly thought to be one of the Three Wise Men; Nebuchadnezzar was the powerful king of Babylon who cast Shadrach, Meshach and Abednego into the fiery furnace and Daniel into the lion's den (they all miraculously lived to tell the tale); Melchior is another of the Three Wise Men or Magi who travelled from the east following the Star of Bethlehem.

This mnemonic may help you remember each bottle in order of size:

M. J. Raps Makes Such Beautiful New Music.

THE RINGS ON THE OLYMPIC FLAG

The five rings are coloured: Black, Yellow, Blue, Green, Red.

The initial letters of each form: BYBGR and Olympic records can be set BY jumping BiGgeR distances.

PORT AND STARBOARD

Port and left both have four letters.

Port is traditionally always passed to the left after dinner.

We Left Port and went Right to Starboard.

The terms port and starboard developed from the earliest days of sailing to avoid any confusion. Starboard is always on the right when facing forwards to the front of the boat. The word comes from the Anglo-Saxon 'steorbord' for rudder.

The Old English for the left-hand side was 'baecbord' although from Medieval times the word 'larboard' was used. This possibly came from 'laddebord' meaning loading side, as the starboard side with its rudder would always have been kept away from the quay.

The earliest reference to 'port' as left is found in Admiral Smyth's *The Sailor's Word Book* of 1867, which states, 'The left side of the ship is called port by Admiralty Order, in preference to larboard, as less mistakeable in sound for starboard.'

Port Out Starboard Home

The acronym for POSH, or is it? The probably apocryphal explanation is that 'port out starboard home' was printed on the more expensive P&O tickets for passengers travelling between Britain and India. The thinking being that as both countries are in the northern hemisphere, port-side cabins were mainly in the shade when travelling out to the east and starboard cabins when travelling home to the west. These were the most desirable and therefore expensive cabins, or in other words posh.

Although this is often quoted, it is unlikely. No P&O tickets printed with the phrase have ever been found although many still exist from the period. Also acronyms are largely 20th century in origin, few were popular before that, and in fact the word 'acronym' itself wasn't used until the 1940s.

THE LAW

Contracts

OAC

Offer, Acceptance, Consideration.

Torts

'Death Before Dishonour!' Cried Rick.

Duty, Breach of duty, Damage, and Causation that is not too Remote.

BASIC SAFETY

Crossing the Road

The immediate danger for pedestrians crossing UK roads comes from traffic approaching from the right. Therefore basic safety rules suggest you should look to the right first and recheck before stepping out. The Green Cross Code, as taught to generations of schoolchildren, reminds us to:

Look right, look left, then right again.

First Aid

A St John Ambulance first aid lesson for two of us roped in to be first aid reps for our floor in one of my first jobs taught me a simple mnemonic for recalling the correct order of response after an accident.

DRAB

Danger, Response, Airways, Breathing.

Danger – assess the situation and any new threats or remaining dangers. For instance, following a car accident, make sure there is a warning for approaching traffic.

Response – check the vital signs of any victims.

Airways – make sure airways are not blocked, by debris or even their own tongue. If a victim is semi or unconscious, it is often best to lay them on their side in the recovery position with the lower arm stretched out and one knee bent.

Breathing – check the victim can breathe by themselves: if not, consider mouth-to-mouth resuscitation.

The word drab is also useful for reminding you to behave in a calm unexcited manner.

Sports injuries

For sports injuries, and especially for suspected fractures, sprains, muscle strains and contusions, remember:

RICE

For 1) Rest, 2) Ice, 3) Compression, 4) Elevation.

And equally important, to know what to avoid, think of:

HARM

For heat, alcohol, running and massage.

Wasp and Bee Stings

I can remember my mother pondering whether it was vinegar for a wasp sting or ammonia as I stood, finger throbbing, feeling sorry for myself. She could never remember which was right and I've always had the same problem. Until I heard a friend chant:

'Use Ammonia for a Bee sting,
And Vinegar for a Wasp sting.'

She added, 'B follows A and W follows V.'

The A to B, V to W is also useful to anyone knowing their Latin family names as, *Apoidae* are Bees while *Vespidae* are Wasps.

Why does this work? Wasp stings are alkaline, so the vinegar as an acid neutralises the poison. Bee stings are acidic and so ammonia, or more usefully bicarbonate of soda mixed into a paste with water, counters the effects.

Less Basic Safety

Coral and King Snakes

Some King snakes have very similar distinct colour bandings to Coral snakes, making them hard to distinguish. This might not matter except for the fact that while King snakes are harmless, Coral snakes are highly venomous – second only to Rattlesnakes in potency in northern America.

Several rhymes exist to help you tell the difference:

> If red touches black it's OK Jack,
> If red touches yellow, you're a dead fellow.
>
> Red on yellow, kill a fellow,
> Red on black, don't kill Jack.

And somewhat bluntly:
> If yellow follows red,
> You're dead.

I have to say, I'm sure I'd panic long before getting any one of these right!

OPENING SCREW TOP JARS AND BOTTLES

It should be so obvious and yet somehow it's so easy to get confused which way to turn the top to open it. This is also useful when wielding a screwdriver.

Righty tighty; lefty loosey.

What could be more simple?

INVESTING

Here are two rhymes giving advice to investors.

Strategy

Don't buy when the market's sky high
And don't sell at the bottom of a well
For you know the market feeds
On people's fear and greed.
The gurus say buy low, sell high,
Easier said than done say I.
Timing the market may lead to profit
But more often is catastrophic.
Forget the fancy computations,
Theoretical models, and speculations:
Look at the trend
And consider it your truest friend,
The surest way to your weight in gold
Is simply to buy and hold.

Interest Rates

When rates are low,
Stocks will grow;
When rates are high,
Stocks will die.

HEREDITARY TITLES

There are five ranks of peer in the United Kingdom which in descending order are: Duke, Marquess, Earl, Viscount and Baron.

These can easily be remembered by the sentence:

Don't Make Every Visit Boring.

The title Lord is not included as it has various meanings. It is most often used by barons but can be given to the children of dukes and marquesses. It may also be a courtesy title rather than hereditary.

William the Conqueror tried to change the Anglo-Saxon title earl to count, and although he failed, earls' wives are known as countesses. A marchioness is the wife of a marquess and a baronet is a hereditary title although not a peerage, ranking between a baron and a knight.

PEOPLE OF LETTERS

Very occasionally you may find yourself writing a formal letter and wondering just what is the correct order for qualifications and honours? The rule is:

Honour before degree
Degree before MP.

And so you would write, 'Rev. M. Cave, OBE, BSc'.

If Reverend Cave also happened to be an MP you would simply add MP at the very end, 'Rev. M. Cave, OBE, BSc, MP.'

THE LOCI OR JOURNEY SYSTEM

This is one of the oldest and most widely used mnemonic methods, practised from classical times and even taught as part of the traditional school curriculum for many years. It is particularly useful for remembering long lists, enabling you to recall many things easily. The great advantage of this method is that you can begin from any point, which distinguishes it from learning by rote, and this explains why it is so popular with actors, speakers and students studying for exams.

The first record of Loci is through an ancient pamphlet called *Rhetorica ad Herennium*, which was written about 85 BC by an unknown Latin author, although the method itself is likely to pre-date this. Cicero refers to Loci in *De Oratore*, attributing its invention to Simonides of Ceos. The story goes that he was at a dinner with a number of important Greek nobles and thinkers. Luckily for Simonides, he had just stepped outside when the roof of the building collapsed, crushing the diners below. Simonides was able to identify each of the victims by matching them to their position, or locus, at the table.

The method is basically a peg system which uses locations (loci) with which you are very familiar. Who hasn't dashed upstairs to fetch something, only to forget what it is? The simplest way to remember is to return to your original position whereupon you can usually recall exactly what you wanted. Loci works in the same way, except the locations you visit to jog your memory are all in the mind.

Picture your home and imagine walking through it. Begin at the front door and move on into the hallway, through the kitchen to the dining room. The more detail you can give to your images, the better, so for instance, concentrate on the ornate hand-shaped knocker on the front door, the distinct terracotta and ochre patterned tiles in the hallway, the green glass fruit bowl on the kitchen worktop. Choose specific places in your house and in your mind visit each in turn, always in the same order but visualising the journey backwards as well as forwards so that it is fixed firmly in your mind.

The traditional advice is that the mental locations should be well lit, in a definite order and physically fairly evenly spaced and not too far apart. In the sixteenth century, public buildings were usually chosen and the journey was often called a 'memory palace'; this helps to give an idea of the sort of mental image you should be creating for yourself.

If you find visualisation difficult, think especially of shape and texture when choosing your loci. People who are very musical or who have good auditory memory can use sound as an aid, adding a distinctive soundtrack to their journey.

Once you are familiar with your loci you can begin to link each point on your journey with items on a list or chunks of a speech represented by distinct objects or symbols. They can then be easily recalled by imagining you are walking through your home, mentally visiting each of your loci. It should become so easy to visualise that you can start your journey at any point meaning you can remember your list or speech in any order, even backwards. The loci can also be used to remember more than one set of items and can be grouped or chunked into small sets as long as they can be mentally visualised in one glance.

As well as choosing detailed, stimulating loci as a starting point, the images you create should also be as vivid as possible. Humorous or incongruous ones are particularly memorable – in 1584 there was furore in England as the Puritans branded the method impious because it encouraged people to think obscene, sacrilegious thoughts. So what are you waiting for? Let your imagination run riot and surprise yourself at just how accurate your memory can be.

As a simple example, picking ten loci in your house, a combination of rooms and furniture, you may have chosen something like the following:

Letterbox on the front door
Carpet runner in the hallway
The fridge in your kitchen
The mirror above the fireplace in your sitting room
The sitting room sofa
The stair banister rail
The washbasin in your bathroom

The bed in your bedroom
The computer in your study
The bookshelves in the study

And so your mind's journey could be something like this:

The dull brass LETTERBOX with the French word
Lettres engraved on it is set at hip height on the glossy,
scarlet-painted front door. Walking into the hallway,
you step onto the striped terracotta and straw-coloured
CARPET RUNNER and walk to the kitchen where you
see the baby blue, chubby FRIDGE standing in the
corner. Turning, you make your way to the sitting room
where you glance at your reflection in the slightly hazed
MIRROR with the ornate frame which hangs above the
fireplace. Next, you slump comfortably onto the purple,
velvet SOFA. Climbing the stairs you run your hands
over the smooth, polished wooden BANISTER RAIL. In
the bathroom you wash your hands in the WASHBASIN
with the nickel taps. You walk along the landing to your
bedroom and look at your metal-framed BED with its
white duvet and patterned quilt. Work in mind, you
return along the landing to your small study with your
white laptop COMPUTER on your desk and the tall,
overstocked BOOKSHELVES next to the window.

Once your journey is fixed in your mind with each detailed loci in order, you can use it to memorise anything you want from facts for exams, to speeches or lists of information. With practice, this can become an incredibly flexible memory system, its potential limited only by how creative you can be.

Begin simply with an easy list:

Basket
Towel
Shampoo
Pineapple
DVD
Deodorant
Mobile phone
Newspaper
Pens
Bar of chocolate

The idea is to associate each item on the list with a stage of your journey, making it as vivid and memorable as possible. For example:

A wicker shopping basket has been wedged into the large, brass letterbox. You struggle to free it, tugging hard until it suddenly shoots into the hallway, spilling the bright orange towel that was inside out onto the striped carpet runner. You walk into the kitchen where an open bottle of shampoo is lying on its side on top of the fridge, creamy shampoo slowly oozing down the pale blue surface. In the sitting room a large pineapple on the fireplace is reflected in the mirror, mouldering in the heat from the fire. You sit down on the squidgy purple sofa, suddenly uncomfortable as a DVD splinters as you sit on it. Walking upstairs, the normally smooth banister rail is sticky with sickly-smelling deodorant. You go to wash your hands in the washbasin only to find it blocked by a giant mobile phone. Walking to your bedroom you are surprised to find your bed covered by newspaper instead of the usual white duvet and quilt. In the study, your white laptop is scrawled with squiggled pen marks, the pens lying next to it in pools of coloured ink. You look up to see that the bookshelves are stocked with giant bars of chocolate in place of books.

You will find that as you mentally walk through your journey visiting each loci, you will clearly see each item on your list. And what's more, you will still remember them even after a gap of some time.

MEMORY PALACES

With a view to expanding the possibilities for memory offered by the Loci system, you can take the technique to a higher level by adding to your journeys and rooms. You can begin by expanding them within your home – for instance, mentally stepping inside your wardrobe, the understairs' cupboard or even the contents of your fridge. But it can also help to create or add new rooms.

Some experts suggest creating imaginary locations but I think this takes quite a time to really fix in your mind and the temptation is to change or improve details which all gets very confusing. Instead I would recommend choosing somewhere you already know well, preferably somewhere you like which you can mentally access from a door or via a corridor you add to your original loci. Your childhood home, a favourite well-visited museum or gallery, a friend's home or even somewhere you holiday can all work well, just so long as you can picture it vividly and there are plenty of interesting details to use as hooks. If you visit somewhere that appeals, photograph it to permanently fix the minutiae ready to be used later.

At this point you might also find it helpful to add markers every so often. The Ancient Greeks suggested a marker every five loci so that you can easily pick up at any point. The fifth one could be marked by a star with five points, number twelve by a dozen eggs: whatever appeals to you. Classical scholars also thought it important that the loci on your journey were well spaced: they recommended they should be at least 2 metres apart. I don't really think this is necessary just as long as they are distinct.

The addition of extra rooms creating a vast memory palace allows you to keep some rooms as permanent stores for information, poetry and facts you know you want to remember for ever. Your can shut and open the door on them at will and keep them quite separate from anything else you may have stored.

HISTORY

'To be ignorant of what happened before you were born is to be ever a child. For what is man's lifetime unless the memory of past events is woven with those of earlier times?'

Marcus Tullius Cicero

Once I started thinking about history in general I surprised myself at how many different mnemonics I remembered at least in part; they are certainly where my memory for the royal dynasties of England and Henry VIII's wives originates. Historical facts and stories have been the inspiration for many poems and songs, including Monty Python's 'Oliver Cromwell', which contains an amazing amount of detail. It was also clear that 'baddies' generally inspired the most mnemonics, presumably because their stories are more colourful. The resulting rhymes, chants, songs and lines are among the most inventive and lively mnemonics. I also discovered one for the exact date, including the hour, at which prohibition was lifted in Finland – read on to find out more.

PERIODS OF HISTORY

Pupils Eat Grapes Regularly During Morning Registration In Toilets.

Should help with:

Prehistoric, Egyptian, Greek, Roman, Dark Ages, Medieval, Renaissance, Industrial Revolution, Twentieth Century and beyond.

THE SEVEN WONDERS OF THE ANCIENT WORLD

Ebenezer Cobham Brewer (1810-1897) is probably best remembered as the author of *Brewer's Dictionary of Phrase and Fable* which is still in print. He wrote a verse listing the Seven Wonders, though rather confusingly, uses Roman rather than Greek names for goddesses:

The Pyramids first, which in Egypt were laid;
Then Babylon's Gardens, for Amytis made;
Third, Mausolus' Tomb, of affection and guilt;
Fourth, the Temple of Dian, in Ephesus built;
Fifth, Colossus of Rhodes, cast in bronze, to the sun;
Sixth, Jupiter's Statue, by Philidas done;
The Pharos of Egypt, last wonder of old,
Or the Palace of Cyrus, cemented with gold.

That is:

1 The Great Pyramid of Giza.
2 The Hanging Gardens of Babylon in Baghdad.
3 The Tomb of Mausolus at Halicarnassus in Greece
4 The Temple of Diana (or Artemis) at Ephesus.
5 The Colossus of Rhodes.
6 The Statue of Jupiter (or Zeus, which was the Greek name) at Olympia.
7 The Pharos, or Lighthouse, at Alexandria.

The ancient Greeks loved making lists and the Palace of Cyrus is occasionally included as a wonder. According to

Herodotus it was built at Ecbatana, in Persia, on the orders of Deioces.

The earliest lists claim the Ishtar Gate as the seventh wonder. This was the eighth gate to the inner city of Babylon, built by order of King Nebuchadnezzar II, dedicated to the goddess Ishtar. The Gate was replaced by the Lighthouse of Alexandria in the sixth Century.

EGYPTIAN PHAROAHS

The New Kingdom covered the eighteenth, nineteenth and twentieth dynasties of Ancient Egypt from the sixteenth to the eleventh century BC. The period saw the Egyptian Empire at its greatest territorially, stretching from Nubia in the south through the Near East with Egyptian armies fighting the Hittites for control of Syria.

The pharaohs of the first two dynasties of the Egyptian New Kingdom are:

Ahmose I, Amenhotep I, Thutmose I, Thutmose II, Thutmose III, Hatshepsut, Amenhotep II, Thutmose IV, Amenhotep III (the Magnificent king), Akhenaten, Smenhakare, Tutankhamun, Ay, Horemheb (18th Dynasty).

Ramesses I, Seti I, Ramesses II (the Great, also the ruler associated with Moses), Merneptah, Amenemses, Seti II, Merneptah, Siptah, Tausret (19th Dynasty).

Here is a slightly convoluted mnemonic sentence for them:

An Apple That Thinks Thinks Heavily And Thinks All Apples Sometimes Think Apparently Has Really Serious Ramifications Mentally And Saves More Serious Thought.

The ten pharaohs of the 20th dynasty are simpler to learn as you only have to remember two names:

Setnakhte, Rameses III, IV, V, VI, VII, VIII, IX, X, XI.

THE DARK AGES

Knights of the Round Table

I realise that strictly speaking this is not history, but as an enduring element of Dark Age mythology it seems worth including King Arthur's famous Knights of the Round Table.

There are many versions of the legend and different authors disagree about how many knights there actually were but these ten are generally accepted by most:

Lancelot, Galahad, Mark, Mordred, Tristram, Gawain, Palomides, Kay, Tor, Lamorack.

They can be called to mind by:

Lance Gallantly Made Muffins To Give Paul's Kite The Lead.

ENGLISH KINGS AND QUEENS

As with many mnemonics, the origin of the rhyme is not known but it is at least 100 years old, with additions to cover the extra monarchs.

Willie, Willie, Harry, Steve,
Harry, Dick, John, Harry Three,
One Two Three Neds, Richard Two,
Harrys Four Five Six . . . then who?
Edwards Four Five, Dick the Bad,
Harrys twain, Ned Six the lad,
Mary, Bessie, James you ken,
Then Charlie, Charlie, James again . . .
Will and Mary, Anne of Gloria,
Georges (four), Will Four, Victoria,
Edward Seven next, and then came George the Fifth in
   1910 . . .
Ned the Eighth soon abdicated,
So George the Sixth was coronated,
Then number Two Elizabeth . . .
And that's all folks (until her death . . .).

A shortened version for the last few lines following on from Victoria is:

Edward Seven, Georgie Five,
Edward, George and Liz (alive).

Written in full the order of rulers is:

William the Conqueror (I), William II Rufus, Henry I,
Stephen, Henry II, Richard I (the Lionheart), John,
Henry III, Edward I (Longshanks), Edward II, Edward III,
Richard II, Henry IV, Henry V, Henry VI, Edward IV,
Edward V, Richard III, Henry VII, Henry VIII, Edward VI,
Mary I, Elizabeth I, James I (and VI of Scotland), Charles I,
Charles II, James II, William and Mary II, Anne, George I,
George II, George III, George IV, William IV, Victoria,
Edward VII, George V, Edward VIII, George VI,
Elizabeth II.

This sentence can help with the first fourteen:

Working Wives Have Seldom Had Racily Jazzy Hemlines,
Triple E Rubber Hardly Helps.

William the Conqueror

There is also:

William the First was the first of our kings,
Not counting Ethelreds, Egberts and things . . .

King John

And to bring to mind one of our worst monarchs:

Bad, bad, bad King John,
Shamed the throne that he sat upon.
Not a scruple, not a straw, cared this monarch for the law.

KING JOHN

In 1192, Prince John first snatched the throne from his brother, the rather more heroic Richard the Lionheart, who was away on crusade at the time. When Richard returned two years later, John was forced to relinquish the throne.

He finally inherited the crown in 1199 and almost immediately began losing England's foreign territories. He also quarrelled with Pope Innocent III and was excommunicated in 1209. Alongside John's disastrous military campaigns (when the French defeated John's army at the Battle of Bouvines in Flanders in 1214 John was away in Poitou apparently trying to organise a pincer movement) he raised taxes alienating the nobility along with the ordinary people. In 1215 a group of barons forced John to sign Magna Carta, the Great Charter of Freedoms, which gave away a great deal of royal power and effectively paved the way for democratic parliament. Magna Carta arguably influenced the development of constitutional common law and can still be seen reflected in many constitutional documents including the United States Constitution.

John acquired two derogatory nicknames during his lifetime. The first was 'Lackland' because as the youngest of five sons he did not inherit any land from his father, and once king, he lost England's territories to France. The second nickname was 'Soft-sword' on account of his military incompetence. The final indignity came with his death. Fleeing from the invading French, who were largely supported by the English nobility as well as the Pope, John retreated into East Anglia where he lost all his baggage including the Crown Jewels in the marshy region of the Wash. Shortly afterwards, he caught dysentery and died, earning the final insult: 'The king who lost his clothes in the Wash.'

> *Lackland John was a right royal tartar,*
> *'Til he made his mark on Magna Carta.*
> *Ink, seal and paper on Runnymede Green*
> *In Anno Domini twelve fifteen.*

ROYAL DYNASTIES

No Plan Like Yours To Study History Suitably Well.

Norman (1066-1154), Plantagenet (1154-1399), Lancastrian (from 1399), York (from 1461), Tudor (1485-1603), Stuart (1603-1649, 1660-1714), Hanoverian (1714-1901), Saxe-Coburg and Gotha (1901-1917 when the dynasty was renamed), Windsor (from 1917 until the present day).

This is a rather simplified version omitting houses that did not actually become dynasties, namely: Blois 1135-54, Angevin 1154-1216 which effectively became the Plantagenets, and Orange 1689-1702 when William of Orange ruled jointly with Queen Mary Stuart. The dynasty changes back and forth between Lancaster and York during the Wars of the Roses are not reflected, simply the earliest date for the rule of both. It also makes no mention of the Commonwealth, including the

Protectorate of Oliver Cromwell (1653-1658), following the beheading of King Charles I in 1649, which lasted until 1660 when the monarchy was reinstated under King Charles II.

GOLDEN JUBILEE MONARCHS

A golden jubilee celebrates 50 years of a monarch's reign and the present Queen Elizabeth marked hers in 2002 with a tour of the UK and Commonwealth, concerts, a service of thanksgiving and procession along The Mall. Although the idea of an actual ceremony to celebrate seems to have begun with Queen Victoria in 1887, three earlier British monarchs also reached this landmark.

Henry III 1216-1272 (56 years)
Edward III 1327-1377 (50 years)
George III 1760-1820 (59 years)

As each king is a 'third', this line is a helpful reminder:

Vicky victorious and three of the Thirds,
And now there is also Elizabeth Two.

James I reigned England for 22 years from 1603-1625, but was actually King James VI of Scotland for 57 years, 1567-1625.

QUEEN VICTORIA'S GOLDEN JUBILEE

As Queen Victoria celebrated her Golden Jubilee on 20 June 1887 with a sumptuous banquet for 50 European kings and princes, she was blissfully unaware of a plot by Irish republicans to blow up Westminster Abbey during a service of thanksgiving which she was to attend. The plot became known as the Jubilee Plot. Despite this, at the time Queen Victoria was extremely popular and well beloved. At this point she is still the longest-reigning monarch, ascending the throne in 1837 and ruling for 64 years until her death in 1901.

The six wives of Henry VIII

Henry VIII ruled from 1509 until 1547. He was a Renaissance man and his court was a centre for scholarly learning, art and music. Among many notable events including the struggle with Rome and ultimately the separation of the Anglican Church, dissolution of the monasteries and establishment of the monarch as the Supreme Head of the Church of England, Henry is infamous for marrying six wives:

Catherine of Aragon (1485-1536) married 1510. The widow of Henry's older brother Arthur and the mother of Mary I.

Anne Boleyn (1507-1536) married 1533. Anne was maid of honour to Catherine of Aragon and the mother of Elizabeth I.

Jane Seymour (1509-1537) married 1536. Jane was lady-in-waiting to both Catherine and Anne. She died of a fever following the birth of Edward VI. She is buried beside Henry VIII at Windsor Castle.

Anne of Cleves (1515-1557) married 1540. She was the daughter of the Duke of Cleves, in Germany. The marriage was never consummated and after the annulment she was given a generous settlement. Anne outlived all Henry's other wives.

Catherine Howard (1522-1542) married 1540. She was just 22 when Henry had her beheaded for treason as she was found guilty of adultery.

Catherine Parr (1512-1548) married 1542. Henry was actually her third husband and she went on to marry for a fourth time, dying of what at the time was called childbed fever, the same illness which claimed the life of Jane Seymour.

There are several well-known rhymes about his wives:

Kate an' Anne an' Jane,
an' Anne an' Kate again, again.

This recalls their names in order of succession. The second has helped decades of school children remember the usually unfortunate fate of each:

Divorced, beheaded, died.
Divorced, beheaded, survived.

And, finally:

Prince Hal of York to six wives was wedded,
One died, one survived, two divorced and two beheaded.

Or to prompt their surnames:

Arrogant	Bull	Sees	Cleaner's	Hair	Parted
Aragon	Boleyn	Seymour	Cleves	Howard	Parr

And their children:

Mary	Elizabeth	Edward	None	None	None

Henry's reputation for dispensing with his chancellors was not much better than with his wives. Just remember that all four were called Thomas and they conveniently follow in reverse alphabetical order:

Thomas Wolsey
Died on the way to trial
Built Hampton Court

Sir Thomas More
Executed

Thomas Cromwell
Executed

Thomas Cranmer
Survived — though later
burned at the stake by Mary

King Charles I and Oliver Cromwell

There is something about songs that fix words in your head so that years later, when a familiar tune plays, the lyrics spring instantly into your brain unbidden. They're often not totally welcome – who hasn't complained about having an unwanted tune fixed in their mind? But there are times when they can be extremely useful as for instance with this Monty Python song about Oliver Cromwell – packed with facts and details, it's helped a number of fans through history tests and exams.

Oliver Cromwell

The most interesting thing about King Charles, the first
Is that he was 5 foot 6 inches tall at the start of his reign
But only 4 foot 8 inches tall at the end of it because of
Oliver Cromwell, Lord Protector of England Puritan
Born in 1599 and died in 1658 September.

Was at first only MP for Hunting Don, but then he led the
    Ironside Cavalry
At Marston Moor in 1644 and won then he founded the
    New Model Army
And praise be, beat the Cavaliers at Naisby and the King
    fled up North
Like a bat to the Scots.

But under the terms of John Pimm's Solemn League and
    Covenant
The Scots handed King Charles the first, over to
Oliver Cromwell, Lord Protector of England and his warts
Born in 1599 and died in 1658 September.

But alas, oy vay! The disagreement then broke out between
The Presbyterian Parliament and the Military who meant

To have an independent bent and so the 2nd Civil War
   broke out
And the Roundhead ranks faced the Cavaliers at Preston
   Banks
And the King lost again, silly thing, stupid Git.

And Cromwell sent Colonel Pride to purge the House of
   Commons
Of the Presbyterian Royalists leaving behind only the
   rump Parliament
Which appointed a High Court at Westminster Hall to
   indict
Charles, the first for tyranny, ooh! Charles was sentenced
   to death
Even though he refused to accept that the court had
   jurisdiction
Say goodbye to his head.

Poor King Charles laid his head on the block
January 1649, down came the axe and in the silence that
   followed
The only sound that could be heard was a solitary giggle from
Oliver Cromwell, Lord Protector of England, olé
Born in 1599 and died in 1658 September.

Then he smashed Ireland, set up the Commonwealth and
   more
He crushed the Scots at Worcester and beat the Dutch at
   sea in 1653

And then he dissolved the rump Parliament
And with Lambert's consent wrote the instrument of
    Government
Under which Oliver was Protector at last.

By John Cleese (set to music by Chopin)
© John Cleese, Python Monty Pictures

CAUSES OF THE FIRST WORLD WAR

Just ask yourself, what are the four MAIN causes of World War
I?

    Answer: Militarism, Alliance, Imperialism, Nationalism.

KEY DATES

1066 and All That

The Battle of Hastings in 1066
When William the Conqueror started his tricks.

The Hundred Years War

Lasting from 1336-1453 the war actually lasted 117 years.
Interestingly, the number of letters and spaces in Hundred
Years War adds up to 17, so just add 17 to 100.

    It was begun by Edward III in a bid for complete sovereignty
over the duchy of Aquitaine in South West France. The war
escalated under Henry V into an attempt to conquer the whole
of France leading to such memorable battles as Agincourt on

St Crispin's Day, 25 October 1415, and the appearance of Joan of Arc as France's saviour at the Siege of Orleans in 1429 (she was burned at the stake at Rouen in 1431 at the age of 19 and finally canonised in 1920).

The Fire of London

The Fire began in Thomas Farynor's bakery in Pudding Lane, close to London Bridge, shortly after midnight on Sunday 2 September 1666. It blazed on through great swathes of the city until it was finally quenched on Wednesday 5 September. Much of the medieval City of London within the old Roman walls was destroyed, although the West End, Westminster and Charles II's palace at Whitehall escaped the flames.

It is possible that more of the city could have been saved if the widescale demolitions suggested by firefighters had been carried out sooner. The Lord Mayor, Sir Thomas Bloodworth, was blamed for the delay, famously remarking about the blaze, 'Pish! A woman could piss it out.' Samuel Pepys wrote in detail about the events in his diary, commenting, 'It made me weep to see it.'

Despite many radical plans for rebuilding, the city was largely reconstructed on the original street plan which existed before the fire.

1666 can be represented by a simple diagram showing the 6s as chimneys with smoke rising.

Or, I think easier to bring to mind:

In sixteen hundred and sixty-six,
London burned like rotten sticks.

Nelson and Napoleon

Vice-Admiral Horatio Nelson defeated Napoleon on 21 October 1805 at the Battle of Trafalgar, during which he was killed. He was also injured during several earlier battles, losing both his right eye (the 1794 capture of Corsica) and right arm (in the 1797 Battle of Santa Cruz). The order in which he sustained his injuries can be remembered simply by the word:

EARS

(Eye, Arm — both Rights)

After the Battle of Trafalgar, Napoleon was defeated at the Battle of Toulouse in 1814 after which he was exiled to the island of Elba. A well-known palindrome records this:

Able was I ere I saw Elba.

Napoleon actually escaped from Elba and was finally defeated by Wellington at the Battle of Waterloo in 1815, after which he was exiled to the far Atlantic island of St Helena, where he died in 1821.

American History

The discovery of the New World

In fourteen hundred and ninety-two, Columbus sailed the ocean blue.

The Original 13 States

This is a useful mnemonic for remembering the 13 original colonies of the US:

Cory Doesn't Give My Mom's Nutty New Noisy Neighbour
Pam Rides In Sister's Van.

Connecticut, Delaware, Georgia, Massachusetts, Maryland, New Hampshire, New York, New Jersey, North Carolina, Pennsylavania, Rhode Island, South Carolina, Virginia.

Paul Revere

Baptised on 1 January 1735 and died on 10 May 1818, Paul Revere was a silversmith and American patriot, celebrated after his death for his role as messenger in the battles of Lexington and Concord in the American Revolutionary War.

His famed 'Midnight Ride' took place on the night of 18–19 April 1775 when he and William Dawes were asked to ride from Boston to Lexington to warn John Hancock and Samuel Adams of the movement of the British Army who were planning to seize the weapons store in Concord and at the same time arrest Hancock and Adams. The poem was written by the American Henry Wadsworth Longfellow in 1860 and tells the fictionalised story of Revere as narrated by the landlord of the Wayside Inn.

> *Now listen my children and you shall hear*
> *Of the midnight ride of Paul Revere.*
> *On the eighteenth of April in Seventy-Five;*
> *Hardly a man is now alive*
> *Who remembers that famous day and year.*

The poem goes on to relate the heroic events of the night, but in fact Revere and Dawes were joined by Dr Samuel Prescott on the road and were then stopped by British troops at Lincoln. Dawes and Prescott escaped while Revere was escorted at gunpoint back to Lexington. Of the three, only Prescott actually arrived in Concord in time to warn the American militia.

And if you are concerned to remember William Dawes who initially set out with Revere you might like Helen F. Moore's parody of Longfellow, written in 1896:

> *'Tis all very well for the children to hear*
> *Of the midnight ride of Paul Revere;*
> *But why should my name be quite forgot,*
> *Who rode as boldly and well, God wot?*
> *Why should I ask? The reason is clear —*
> *My name was Dawes and his Revere.*

Did you know?

On 4 July 1826, the 50th anniversary of the founding of the United States, both the second (John Adams) and third

(Thomas Jefferson) Presidents died within a few hours of each other.

US Presidents

To remember the first presidents, just ask yourself:

Will A Jolly Man Make A Just But Harshly Treated President?

Washington, Adams, Jefferson, Madison, Monroe, (Quincy) Adams, Jackson, Van Buren, Harrison, Tyler, Polk.

The middle US presidents can be recalled:

Taylor Felt Proud But Lincoln Just Grinned, Happily Gargling, And Could Hardly Contain McKinley.

Taylor, Fillmore, Pierce, Buchanan, Lincoln, Johnson, Grant, Hayes, Garfield, Arthur, Cleveland, Harrison, Cleveland, McKinley.

Or if you prefer, for the first 14 presidents:

When A Joke Made Me A Joker, Van Had To Poke The Fiery Poker.

Washington, Adams, Jefferson, Madison, Monroe, (Quincy) Adams, Jackson, Van Buren.

The 20th Century using several of their names:

Theodore Takes Wilson's Hand Coolly Hoovering Franklin's True Experiences. Ken, Justly Noted For Candour, Rules But Calmly.

Theodore Roosevelt, Taft, Wilson, Harding, Coolidge, Hoover, Franklin D. Roosevelt, Truman, Eisenhower, Kennedy, Johnson, Nixon, Ford, Carter, Reagan, Bush, Clinton.

The complete list with the dates of their presidencies is:

1   George Washington 1789-1797
2   John Adams 1797-1801
3   Thomas Jefferson 1801-1809
4   James Madison 1809-1817
5   James Monroe 1817-1825
6   John Quincy Adams 1825-1829 (the first President who was also the son of a President)
7   Andrew Jackson 1829-1837
8   Martin Van Buren 1837-1841
9   William Henry Harrison 1841 (in office less than a month, he caught a cold and died of pneumonia on 4 April, the first president to die in office)
10 John Tyler 1841-1845 (dubbed 'his Accidency', he was the first vice-president to become president following the death of his predecessor)
11 James K. Polk 1845-1849
12 Zachary Taylor 1849-1850 (fell ill and died after the Fourth of July ceremonies)
13 Millard Fillmore 1850-1853
14 Franklin Pierce 1853-1857
15 James Buchanan 1857-1861
16 Abraham Lincoln 1861-1865 (on Good Friday, 14 April

1865, Lincoln was assassinated by the actor John Wilkes, who mistakenly thought his action would help the South)

17 Andrew Johnson 1865-1869

18 Ulysses S. Grant 1869-1877

19 Rutherford B. Hayes 1877-1881

20 James Garfield 1881 (on 2 July 1881, Garfield was shot by an embittered attorney, he lay wounded for weeks, dying on 19 September)

21 Chester Alan Arthur 1881-1885

22 and 24 Grover Cleveland 1885-1889, 1893-1897 (the first Democrat to be elected after the Civil War and the only president to leave office and return for a second term four years later)

23 Benjamin Harrison 1889-1893

24 Grover Cleveland 1893-1897

25 William McKinley 1897-1901 (his second term as president came to a sad end when he was shot by an anarchist in September 1901)

26 Theodore Roosevelt 1901-1909 (at 43 he became the youngest president thus far)

27 William H. Taft 1909-1913

28 Woodrow Wilson 1913-1921 (he took the United States into the First World War in 1917)

29 Warren G. Harding 1921-1923

30 Calvin Coolidge 1923-1929

31 Herbert Hoover 1929-1933

32 Franklin D. Roosevelt 1933-1945

33   Harry S. Truman 1945-1953
34   Dwight D. Eisenhower 1953-1961
35   John Fitzgerald Kennedy 1961-1963 (the youngest man
     to be elected president and the youngest to die in office.
     He had just passed 1000 days in office when he was
     assassinated in Dallas, Texas on 22 November 1963)
36   Lyndon B. Johnson 1963-1969
37   Richard M. Nixon 1969-1974 (infamous for the
     Watergate scandal)
38   Gerald Ford 1974-1977
39   Jimmy Carter 1977-1981
40   Ronald Reagan 1981-1989
41   George H. W. Bush 1989-1993
42   Bill (William) Jefferson Clinton 1993-2001
43   George W. Bush 2001-2009
44   Barack H. Obama 2009 -

The Presidential Heads Carved on Mount Rushmore

We Just Like Rushmore.

George Washington, Thomas Jefferson, Abraham Lincoln, Theodore Roosevelt.

Mount Rushmore National Memorial near Keystone, South Dakota, was carved by the sculptor Gutzon Borglum. It represents the first 150 years' history of the United States with 18-metre-high sculptures of the four presidents.

Confederate States

To recall the order of secession of the Confederate States of America after the civil war, think of:

So My Father Ate Grapes Last Tuesday, Very Awesome Tart Napas.

South Carolina,
Mississippi,
Florida,
Alabama,
Georgia,
Louisiana,
Texas.

The comma in the sentence represents Lincoln's call for troops after which four further states seceded:

Virginia,
Arkansas,
Tennessee,
North Carolina.

PROHIBITION

Prohibition refers to a law banning the manufacture, sale and transportation, including the import and export, of alcohol to drink. The term is usually taken to refer to the laws passed during the first half of the twentieth century as a result of pressure from Protestant temperance movements warning against the evils of alcohol.

It was most famously enforced in the United States from October 28 1919 until the Great Depression when President Franklin D. Roosevelt amended the law allowing the manufacture and sale of certain types of alcoholic drink on 23 March 1933. The law was finally repealed on 5 December of that year. However, the US was not the only country to pass laws of prohibition as the Temperance Movement was also particularly strong in Scandinavia:

1900 to 1948 Prince Edward Island and other parts of Canada for shorter periods
1914 to 1925 Russia and the USSR
1915 to 1922 Iceland (beer remained banned until 1989)
1916 to 1927 Norway
1919 Hungary
1919 to 1932 Finland

There is a rather neat, though probably not very useful, mnemonic for the exact date that prohibition was lifted in Finland:

543210

The 5th of the 4th month in 1932 at 10 in the morning.

THE PEG AND MAJOR SYSTEMS – THE NUMBER/RHYME MNEMONIC

The Peg System uses numbers instead of words and is particularly useful for learning anything involving figures – telephone numbers, bank accounts, PIN codes, dates, or any of the other numbers we can struggle to remember correctly every day.

To work the system you must memorise a list of words which are easy to associate with the numbers they represent. Generally the list only has to be memorised once, after which it can be used many times. It is usually easiest to remember the words if they rhyme. So your list could go something like this:

One	Gun
Two	Shoe
Three	Tree
Four	Door
Five	Hive
Six	Sticks
Seven	Heaven
Eight	Gate
Nine	Wine
Ten	Pen

Although this is very easy to remember, it is limited in the number of pegs it can produce. Rhyming is also more difficult once you reach the teens and above. You can over-come this by repeating the same images in each group of ten, so for instance 15, 25, 35, 45, 55, etc can all be hives with bees, but each group of ten can be represented differently so 11-20 could be hot and sunny, 21-30 snowy cold, 31-40 red, 41- 50 green and so on. However, this would obviously quickly become very complex.

The Major System develops the Peg System further making it possible to remember much longer numbers. It works by converting each number into a consonant sound and then into words by adding vowels. The words are more easily remembered than the numbers, especially if you make sure the words themselves are memorable as you would with any other memory system.

Digits from 0 to 9 are represented by different consonants, the choice of letters dictated by those we most readily connect with each number. Vowels and the letters w, h and y are not assigned to a particular digit and can be used as fillers to make up useful words. The choice of consonants varies and you can draw up your own, but the most popular list is:

Digit	Letters	Explanation
0	s/z	z is the first letter of zero and s is the most similar in sound.

Digit	Letters	Explanation
1	d/t	both have only one downstroke and the letters sound similar.
2	n	n has two downstrokes.
3	m	m has three downstrokes.
4	r	r is the last letter of four, plus 4 and R have similarities.
5	l	In Roman numerals, L is 50.
6	j/g, sh and soft ch	j has a lower loop and g is similar to a 6 flipped over, sh and ch sound similar.
7	k, hard c, q	Capital K contains two 7s, hard c and q sound similar.
8	f/v, th	an old-fashioned f resembles an 8 and v sounds similar; th because of the 'ht' in eight.
9	b/p	p can be seen as a mirror image of 9 and b sounds similar and also has a resemblance to a flipped 9.

When using the system, it is the consonant sound that matters, not the spelling: for example, action would stand for 762, while enough would be 28 as the 'gh' sounds like 'f'.

If this memory system appeals to you, the first thing to do is to read through several times to make sure that it all makes sense to you. Don't be afraid to make changes to suit yourself: mind trick expert Derren Brown uses f and v to represent the number five and ch/sh/j for eight. Once you are happy with your list familiarise yourself with it and memorise it – read through slowly, write it out again, then turn the page over and check whether you can remember them all.

Now take things a step further and practise using it. A good place to start is by turning your PIN codes into words. Using the letters above, 9220 could become 'bananas', while 7510 could be 'Celts'. Once you're happy with this, move on to longer telephone numbers. Remember to add in vowel sounds and the letters w, h, y to make several words or a sentence. The telephone number 0141 342 020 could become 'Saturday morn snooze', for instance, or you may find you prefer a sequence of images reflecting the person whose phone number it is.

The Major system works particularly effectively when combined with other mnemonic techniques such as rhyming or memorable imagery, and with both the Peg and Loci systems. As always, the more familiar you are with the system and the more you use it, the more skilful you will become and the better your memory will appear.

TIME
AND CALENDARS

'We cross our bridges when we come to them and burn them behind us, with nothing to show for our progress except a memory of the smell of smoke, and a presumption that once our eyes watered.'

TOM STOPPARD

Time and calendars have inspired some of our best-known and oldest mnemonics, including one about the number of days in the months which is familiar to most people. A few have known authors but most are of unknown origin.

CLOCKS FORWARD AND BACK

Spring forward, Fall back.

We now think of fall as the American name for autumn, but in fact it was an Elizabethan term which must have travelled across the Atlantic with the Founding Fathers.

There is also another once popular rhyme:

> *Forward April, back September,*
> *That is all you need to remember.*

However, this could be confusing as British Summer Time is actually set from late March to late October, usually beginning after the third Saturday in March and lasting until the fourth Sunday in October. It seems that every year the resetting of the clocks prompts a wave of debate, but the introduction of British Summer Time is fairly recent, beginning in 1917.

DAYS IN THE MONTH

30 days hath September,
April, June and November.
All the rest have 31
Except February alone,
Which has 28 days clear
And 29 in each leap year.

Alternatively, you can use your hands:
Excluding your thumbs, tap the knuckles and spaces in between so that January is high, February low, March high, April low. When you run out of knuckles on one hand, start again on the second with high August, low September and so on. The months where you have tapped a low have fewer days than the high months, which all have 31.

THE FOUR SEASONS

For clues to the official date when each season begins, remember that all start on the 20-something of the month and then count the number of vowels in each season's name.

Season	No. of Vowels	Start date
sprIng	1	21 March
sUmmEr	2	22 June
AUtUmn	3	23 September
wIntEr	2	22 December

To help fix the months, remember that the shortest day and the start of winter is just three days before Christmas and that the seasons change every quarter year, or each three months.

QUARTER DAYS

Quarter Days were the four dates in the English calendar when rents were traditionally due. As with the four seasons, all are the 20-something of the month:

25 March, or Lady Day – *There are five letters in March*
24 June, Midsummer Day – *Remember, four letters in June*
29 September, Michaelmas Day – *Nine letters in September*
25 December, Christmas Day – *I'm assuming this needs no prompt*

Under the old-style, or Julian calendar which was used in Britain from 46 BC until the mid-18th century, new year began on Lady Day in March. In 1752 Britain adopted the new style, Gregorian calendar to bring it in line with the rest of Europe where it had been used since the 16th century.

By 1752, however, Britain had lost 11 days by staying with the inaccurate Julian Calendar and in that year these were simply skipped, so the 2 September was followed by the 14 September. Some things never change though and the Treasury refused to accept the loss of 11 days' taxes. The missing days were tacked onto the end of the legal year, which had been Lady Day since the Middle Ages. This is the reason why our tax year still begins on 6 April.

SIGNS OF THE ZODIAC

The zodiac is usually taken to refer to the annual cycle of 12 signs marking the sun's elliptic path. It is derived from ancient Babylonian and Greek astronomy and was certainly used in Roman times and is described in Ptolemy's *Almagest*, written in the 2nd century AD. The zodiac remains the basis of the elyptic coordinate system which is still used in astronomy.

Think of this mnemonic for the names of all 12 signs in order:

A Timid Grey Cat Lay Very Low, Skulking Slowly,
Contemplating A Pigeon.

Aries, Taurus, Gemini, Cancer, Leo, Virgo, Libra, Scorpio, Sagittarius, Capricorn, Aquarius, Pisces.

Ebenezer Cobham Brewer (of *Brewer's Dictionary of Phrase and Fable* fame) wrote a verse describing the symbols for each constellation rather than the name in most cases. Again beginning with Aries in the spring:

> Our vernal signs the Ram begins,
> Then comes the Bull, in May the Twins;
> The Crab in June, next Leo shines,
> And Virgo ends the northern signs.
>
> The Balance brings autumnal fruits,
> The Scorpion stings, the Archer shoots;
> December's Goat brings wintry blast,
> Aquarius rain, the Fish comes last.

IDES AND NONES

Before the adoption of the Julian calendar in 46 BC, the Romans are believed to have used a lunar calendar, possibly based on a more ancient Greek version. This involved counting backwards from three fixed points in the following month, the Nones, the Ides and the Kalends. This rhyme has helped classical scholars:

> In March, July, October, May,
> The Ides are on the 15th day,
> The Nones the 7th, but all besides
> Have two days less for Nones and Ides.

THE ALPHABET TECHNIQUE

Like the Number/Rhyme system, the Alphabet Technique is a pegword memory system using the letters of the alphabet in place of numbers. It works by creating images for each letter and then linking them to items on the list you want to remember. Because the alphabet is so ingrained in our minds, at its most basic, this technique can be a good way of learning longer lists in order and in a way that makes it obvious if anything is missing. It is more sophisticated than the number/ rhyme system but rather more difficult to learn and can seem unnecessarily complicated. Tony Buzan, in his book *Use Your Perfect Memory* suggests concentrating on the phonetic sound of the letter rather than the letter itself, so for instance, the letter 'k' is represented by a cake rather than a kite.

As with all such memory techniques it is important that the images work for you, so don't be afraid to play around and change them.

Here is the image scheme that's most frequently used but feel free to go with the picture that has the strongest connection for you:

A	Ace of spades	F	Effluent
B	Bee	G	Jeans
C	Sea	H	H-bomb, itch
D	Diesel engine	I	Eye
E	Eagle	J	Jade

K	Cake	S	Eskimo
L	Elephant	T	Teapot
M	Empty	U	Unicycle
N	Entrance	V	Vehicle
O	Oboe	W	WC
P	Pea	X	X-ray
Q	Queue	Y	Wire
R	Ark	Z	Zulu

© *Use Your Perfect Memory*, Tony Buzan, BBC Worldwide Limited

Take some time to assimilate these images for each letter until you are completely familiar with them. Next, you should try associating items on a list with each letter. At this point I should admit that this is not a technique that really works for me. I find that it takes me such a long time to think of imaginative but workable ways to link images to each letter that for me it's quicker to just learn the list by reading and rereading. But it really does work well for many people and experts.

Often quoted examples of the alphabet technique use the names of famous philosophers:

A – the Ace of spades stands for Freud: a smoking ace is lifted from a Frying pan where it has been well FRiED.

G – Jeans stands for Nietsche: a worn pair of Jeans has a Knee showing through.

H – H-bomb recalls Kafka: a bomb explodes a dismal, grey official café.

THE BIBLE/SUNDAY SCHOOL

'Science without religion is lame, religion without science is blind.'

ALBERT EINSTEIN

I can remember learning 'Matthew, Mark, Luke and John, Bless the bed that I lie on' at Sunday School in what amounted to a Nissen hut left over from World War II. I know I was very young because the fairly small upright piano appeared huge to me then. In my mind the verse is completely tied up with the songs, 'The wise man built his house upon the rock,' and 'I will make you fishers of men,' except that at the time I heard it as 'fishy an' men' which puzzled me.

The Twelve Disciples

The Ignatian *Faith and Life* manual sets them out like this, relying on the similarities between a handwritten, script J and I:

Bartholomew
Andrew
Peter, Philip
Thomas, Thaddaeus (also known as Judas)
John, James, James, Judas Iscariot
Simon
Matthew

Or: Bart and John fill Tom's Mat
        With two Jams, two Juds, and two Simons.

And: This is the way the disciples run:
        Peter, Andrew, James and John,
        Philip and Bartholomew
        Thomas next and Matthew, too,
        James the less and Judas the greater,
        Simon the Zealot and Judas the traitor.

You've probably noticed a certain discrepancy as the names of
the twelve vary between the Gospels. They are generally listed
as:

Simon (named Peter by Jesus) and his brother Andrew,
    who were both fishermen
James and John, sons of Zebedee (given the name
    Boanerges, or Sons of Thunder) who were also
    fishermen
Philip
Bartholomew
Thomas (sometimes referred to as 'doubting' Thomas)
Matthew the tax collector
James son of Alphaeus (the lesser James)
Simon the Cananaean, also known as the Zealot
Judas (the greater) son of James (according to Luke) or
    Thaddaeus (according to Matthew and Mark)
Judas Iscariot

The Books of the Bible

The Old Testament

There are 39 books in the Old Testament and there's no point in pretending there's an easy way to learn them all. But there is a poem of unknown age and origin which can really help if you enjoy rhyme, and if you want to practise any of the memory techniques, this is the ideal list to peg to the Number/rhyme mnemonic or Major System.

The great Jehovah speaks to us
In **Genesis** and **Exodus**;
Leviticus and **Numbers** see,
Followed by **Deuteronomy**.
Joshua and **Judges** sweep the land,
Ruth gleans a sheaf with trembling hand;
Samuelx2 and numerous **Kings**x2 appear,
Whose **Chronicles**x2 we wondering hear.

Ezra and **Nehemiah** now,
Esther the beauteous mourner show,
Job speaks in sighs, David in **Psalms**,
The **Proverbs** teach us to scatter alms.

Ecclesiastes then comes on,
And the sweet **Song of Solomon**.
Isaiah, **Jeremiah** then
With **Lamentations** takes his pen.

Ezekiel, **Daniel**, **Hosea**'s lyres,
Swell **Joel**, **Amos**, **Obadiah**'s.
Next **Jonah**, **Micah**, **Nahum** come,
And lofty **Habbakuk** finds room.

While **Zephaniah**, **Haggai** calls,
Rapt **Zechariah** builds his walls,
And **Malachi** with garments rent,
Concludes the ancient testament.

This sentence is an extra aid for the first five books:

God's Exalted Love Never Dies.

The Four Gospels

Many people will remember from childhood:

Matthew, Mark, Luke and John,
Went to bed with their trousers on.

And the prayer:

Matthew, Mark, Luke and John
Bless the bed that I lie on.
If I die before I wake,
I pray dear Lord my soul to take.

The Books of the New Testament

There are 27 books in the New Testament: think back to the 39 in the Old Testament, or, usefully, the letters of New (3) and Testament (9) and simply multiply 3 by 9.

The books are usually broken into chunks with sentences to prompt your memory:

Matthew	Corinthians 1 and 2
Mark	Galatians
Luke	Ephesians
John	Philippians
Acts	Colossians
Romans	

Matthew, Mark, Luke and John, Act Rather too Corny at the General Electric Power Company.

Or assuming it's fairly easy to remember Matthew, Mark, Luke, John, Acts, you can then use:

Roosters Can Crow, Geese Eat Pop Corn, Turkeys Trot.

For: Romans, Corinthians 1 and 2, Galatians, Ephesians, Philippians, Colossians and Thessalonians 1 and 2 from the next section.

It's also useful to bear in mind that all the books beginning with a 'T' come together in the New Testament:

Thessalonians 1 and 2	Philemon
Timothy 1 and 2	Hebrews
Titus	

Then The Timothys Taught Titus Philemon's Hebrew.

James	Jude
Peter 1 and 2	Revelation
John 1,2 and 3	

James, two Peters, three Johns and one Jude found Revelation.

The Seven Deadly Sins

The named seven have changed and developed somewhat over the centuries and if you look at Galatians chapter 5 you will find a much longer list. However, it is now usually agreed to be:

Wrath, Avarice, Gluttony, Sloth, Pride, Lust, Envy.

We All Gain Semi Professional Leaders Easily.

Or you can take each initial to make either WASP LEG or PAW LEGS.

The Virtues

The seven corresponding virtues are:

Humility, Charity, Kindness, Temperance, Chastity, Diligence, Patience.

Which can be remembered by:

Humorous Clare Kindly Takes Charge During Parties.

Or from 1 Corinthians 13 v.13 the four traditional Christian virtues of, Faith, Hope, Charity and Love, which are probably more easily remembered than the sentence:

Flowers Hopefully Chase Light.

There are also the fruits of the spirit as outlined in Galatians 5: 22-23:

'But the fruit of the Spirit is love, joy, peace, patience, kindness, goodness, faithfulness, gentleness and self-control.'

USING YOUR SENSES

'... the smell and taste of things remain poised a long time, like souls bearing resiliently on tiny and almost impalpable drops of their essence, the immense edifice of memory.'

MARCEL PROUST

There are three basic steps in the creation of memories: sensory memory, short-term memory and long-term memory. Information is first absorbed by the sensory memory which holds an exact copy but only for a few seconds. The information is then transferred to the short-term memory which is sometimes more usefully called the working memory. It is this working memory which is sometimes disrupted in dyslexics, making it hard for them to process and assimilate lots of messages quickly. Psychologist George Miller calculates that the short-term memory can hold seven bits of information plus or minus two. 'Bits' are basically units such as numbers, phrases or words. The last stage involves the transfer of information into long-term memory, probably in the hippocampus where it is organised for easy retrieval.

The senses are always involved to a degree in memory. Who hasn't caught a particular smell whether newly mown grass, fresh coffee or even sun cream and been instantly transported to another time and place? Taste can do the same, Proust was not alone in his appreciation of a madeleine, and sound is just as compelling: when using the Loci System, many people find it improves their recall if they add distinct sound effects or music. But for some people, their senses add an extra element to the way they remember and recall information.

MEMORY AND COLOUR

The American Psychological Society is just one organisation which has reported on the influence of colour on memory.

During a demonstration to show the limits of human memory, university student were read four lists of nine numbers. Afterwards, most people could recall six, seven or occasionally eight of the numbers in each list but at the end of the class, about 2 hours later, one 21-year-old could recall all four lists of digits. Not only that, but when paid a surprise visit 2 months later, she could still remember them perfectly.

Why was she able to recall the numbers so easily? For her, each number had a specific colour or photism and it was the colours that made the digits so easy to remember.

This ability is called 'digit-colour synesthesia' and in common with other synesthetes, this student's digit-colour matchings did not change over time and they happen automatically. This is now a fairly well documented phenomena, another famous case being the professional mnemonist Shereshevsky, in the 1960s, who was also a synesthete. After studying 50 digits for three minutes he was able to remember them all even many years later.

MEMORY AND MUSIC

Learning to read music and play an instrument can help children improve their language skills and may even aid recovery in cases of memory loss following brain injury. Psychologists at the Chinese University in Hong Kong studied a group of schoolboys aged six to fifteen and found that those learning an instrument could recall significantly more words when tested than their non-musical counterparts. The same results were found when the boys were retested after 30 minutes. It seems the longer the boys had been learning an instrument, the more words they remembered. Interestingly the findings only applied to words, not images. The findings echoed an earlier study of girls where musical students out-performed non-musical by 16% in verbal tests.

SONGS AS MNEMONICS

There's no doubt that songs help you learn, sometimes even when you don't want to. Most people can remember words to songs they heard years ago, even when they dislike the song. Snatches of tunes play through your brain whether you want them to or not and are sometimes hard to shift.

At their most basic level, songs are a simple mnemonic device that help you learn and memorise information. It seems they tap into a primitive part of our brain. Music prompts our memory for words, resonating with our ancient roots. Music, song and speech were always part of our communication with one another, just as animals use sound and song to communicate. It's easy to forget that long stories, verses and poems were learned by heart to be recited or sung with ease at a time before print became commonplace and few people could read. Speech and song are part of our oral and aural tradition.

The rhymes and verses also naturally break material into chunks which are easier for our brains to code and store. As children we learn our first songs using rhyme and tunes to help us remember.

Neurobiological research has established a close link between the brain's hearing and emotional centres. Dr Mark Tramo, Director of the Institute for Music and Brain Science at Harvard, says, 'The connectivity of the brain's auditory and emotional systems underlie musical aesthetics,' which helps to explain why music has such a powerful effect on our minds and memories.

We are constantly advised to create an image to establish an emotional connection with the information we want to remember. With music we don't need to try: the connection is already there.

MEMORY, SMELL AND TASTE

'For the sense of smell, almost more than any other,
has the power to recall memories and it is a pity
that you use it so little.'

RACHEL CARSON

Scents and tastes instantly evoke a wave of memories which can influence our mood and performance. From an evolutionary perspective, these two senses are our most important and link directly to the most primitive part of our brain, the home of instinct and memory. As with all mammals, it is through smell and taste that we recognise food and poison: those things which will nourish us and those which will make us ill, fundamental to our basic survival.

Humans have around a thousand scent receptors or sensors in their noses and can identify something like 10,000 different smells. Each sensor recognises several smells and in turn, a single smell is recognised by several different receptors. Associate Professor at Harvard Linda Buck likens this system to individual letters being used in various combinations to make words.

The scent molecule enters the nose where it is recognised by scent receptors which send signals to the olfactory bulb in the brain, just above the eyes. From there, signals are sent to both the limbic system and the olfactory part of the cortex. The limbic system is the primitive part of the brain so closely

CREATING
A MEMORABLE RANDOM PASSWORD

It's so easy to fall into the habit of using the same password for everything which, if you believe all the warnings, can leave you vulnerable to identity fraud.

To choose a password which appears completely random but is also easy to remember, try this: Make up a sentence which you commit to memory and simply use the first letter of each word as your passcode. It is also easy to build numbers into this. For example:

I Watched The Northern Lights In September 08 In Lapland.

Which gives you an 11-digit password including two numbers: IWTNLISo8IL

---

associated with memory, feelings and behaviour that it is sometimes called the 'emotional' brain. The cortex is in the outer part of the brain that is concerned with conscious thought. The signals also travel to the taste sensory cortex to create a sense of taste.

Although sensory neurons only survive for about two months, smells and tastes can bring back distant memories. This is because new olfactory neurons are constantly generated and signals from particular receptors always go to the same place.

Trygg Engen, a psychologist at Brown University in the US, states that smells act as 'index keys' to quickly recall certain memories in our brain which is why smell and taste can trigger more instant and powerful memories than either sight or hearing.

We also have conditioned responses to certain smells and flavours. When you first smell or taste something new you link it with a particular event or person and the brain forges a link. Often these are childhood memories, because we mainly come across new scents and tastes when we are young.

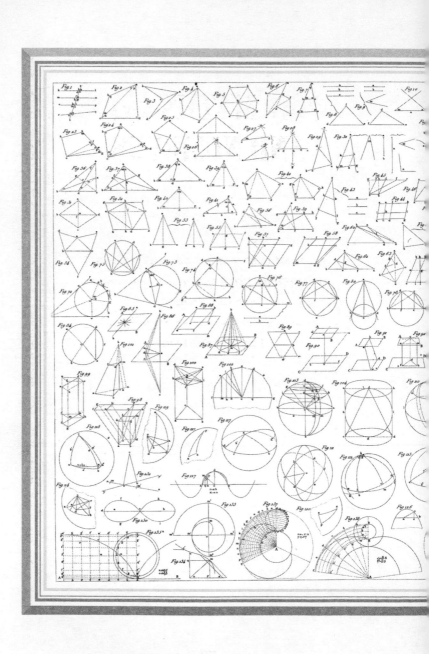

MATHS AND NUMBERS

*Do not worry about your difficulties
in mathematics. I can assure you mine
are still greater.*

ALBERT EINSTEIN

It's only since I left school and didn't need to worry about maths tests and exams any more that I began to appreciate the patterns in numbers and that there really is a symmetry and logic to maths. It is also only recently that I discovered there are many helpful tricks for remembering the rules.

PI

The value of Pi is the ratio of the circumference to the diameter of a circle hence the equation Area = Pi x r squared. There are various sentences using words of different lengths to represent each digit.

The first eight decimal places of Pi:

3. 1 4 1 5 9 2 6

May I have a large container of coffee.

To 13 places:

3. 1 4 1 5 9 2 6 5 3 5 8 9

See, I have a rhyme assisting my feeble brain its tasks sometime resisting.

And to 31 places:

3.1415926535897932384626433832779

Now I, even I, would
Celebrate
In rhymes unapt, the great
Immortal Syracusan, rivalled
Nevermore,
Who in his wondrous lore,
Passed on before,
Left men his guidance
How to circles mensurate.

Or:

Sir, I send a rhyme excelling
In sacred truth and rigid spelling
Numerical sprites elucidate
For me the lexicon's full weight
If nature gain, who can complain
Tho' Doc Johnson fulminate.

This is a mnemonic limerick that not only helps you remember Pi to five decimal places, but also reminds how to calculate the circumference of a circle.

If you cross a circle with a line
Which hits the centre and runs from spine to spine
And the line's length is C
The circumference will be C times 3.14159.

PRIME NUMBERS

Prime numbers are numbers which can only be divided by 1 and themselves. Working on the same principle as the Pi mnemonics, counting the letters of each word in the following sentence gives the first seven prime numbers:

In the early morning, astronomers spiritualised non-mathematicians.

2   3   5   7   11   13   17

The hundredth prime number is 541 and the thousandth, 7919.

THE METRIC SYSTEM

Kilometre hectometre decametre metre decimetre
centimetre millimetre
*King Hector died miserable death —
caught measles.*

This can be slightly adapted as:

King Hector Doesn't Usually Drink Cold Milk.

For:

Kilo	1000	Deci	0.1
Hecto	100	Centi	0.01
Deca	10	Milli	0.001
Units	1		

WEIGHTS AND MEASURES

The weight of water in a UK pint is 20 fluid ounces:

A pint of water
Weighs a pound and a quarter.

But a US pint weighs 16 fluid ounces:

A pint's a pound
In the world around.

And to remember the number of litres in a UK pint:

A litre of water's
A pint and three-quarters.

CALCULUS

The positive quadrants:

All Sine   Tangent Cosine

All students take   calculus.

TRIGONOMETRY

Tan=opposite/adjacent
The old Arab   Cos=adjacent/hypotenuse
          carried a heavy   Sine=opp/hypotenuse
                    sack of hay.

SOHCAHTOA

To remember the three main trigonometric functions:

For Sine you divide Opposite side over Hypotenuse;
for Cosine you divide Adjacent side over Hypotenuse;
for Tangent you divide Opposite side over Adjacent side.

And to remember SOHCAHTOA:

Some Old Horse
Caught A Horse
Taking Oats Away

Or:

Silly Old Harry
Caught A Herring
Trawling Off America

PYTHAGORAS'S THEOREM

The theorem allows pupils to find the length of the third side of a right-angled triangle given the lengths of the other two sides:

'In a right-angled triangle the square of the hypotenuse is equal to the sum of the square of the other two sides.'

Or you may find it easier to remember as:

The squaw on the hippopotamus is equal to the sum of the squaws on the other two hides.

MATHEMATICAL PROBLEMS

Parenthesis Exponents Multipliers Dividers
Adders Subtractors
Please excuse my dear
Aunt Sally.

That is, the order in which you should tackle a maths problem.

Division

Smaller unit into a Larger? Remember they Divide:

Snails Love Dessert.

Larger unit into a Smaller? Remember they will Multiply:

Llamas Slurp Milk.

1 over 7

is .14 28 57
Just learn one
The others are given.

Dividing by Fractions

Just remember this little rhyme:

The number you're dividing by,
Turn upside down and multiply.

So 8/1/2 become 8 x 2/1 = 16

Long Division

The order of operations, divide, multiply, subtract, compare, remainder can be remembered by:

Does Mcdonald's Sell Cheeseburgers Raw?

Or you may prefer:

Dad, Mum, Sister and Brother, for

Divide, multiply, subtract and bringdown.

Multiplication

Minus times minus is plus,
The reason for this we need not discuss.

Even times even is even,
Even times odd is even,
But odd times odd is always odd.

Numerator over the denominator *becomes:*

Nice Dog.

Borrowing in subtraction:

Bigger bottom better borrow.

TIMES TABLES

I went to school at a time when it was still common practice to chant times tables every day out loud in class. And I have to say, the method worked with me; well at least I can usually get to the right answer even if it means chanting a few numbers, usually starting from 5 times something to reach it. As it turned out, this was also the method that worked for my daughter who found anything involving numbers an immediate off-switch. For a time, reciting one of the tables, chanting it aloud in a sing-song fashion, was part of our daily walk to school. We'd begin at the park gate and continue until we reached a particular tree which marked the end of that day's session. Kept short, often repeated and made as much fun as possible it didn't seem a chore. But there are also other ways to help learning.

One of the best ways to prompt memory is to look for the patterns in the times tables.

2 Times

This is really just a case of doubling the number you are multiplying by:

$2 \times 2 = 4, 2 \times 3 = 6, 2 \times 4 = 8, 2 \times 5 = 10, 2 \times 6 = 12$ and so on.

And once you know your 2 times table you also know 3 x 2, 4 x 2 etc, so you are beginning to learn other tables.

3 Times

If you add the digits in the 3 times table they always make 3 or a multiple of 3:

3   6   9   12   15   18   21   24   27   30   33   36

5 Times

The 5 times table alternately ends in 0 or 5 and it is also always half of 10 times a number, which is the easiest times table of all to learn.

6 Times

When multiplying 6 by an even number, just remember that both the even number and the answer end in the same digit:

6 x 2 = 12, 6x 4 = 24, 6 x 6 = 36, 6 x 8 = 48

8 Times

Beginning with 8, the units always descend in 2s throughout this table:

8   16   24   32   40   48   56   64   72   80   88   96

9 Times

This times table contains several distinct patterns:

9   18   27   36   45   54   63   72   81   90   99   108

As the tens go up, the units go down – 9, 8, 7, etc. Another prompt is the fact that the tens number is always one less than the number you are multiplying by, so:

9 x 2 = 18, 9 x 5 = 45, 7 x 9 = 63, 9 x 9 = 81

And, if you add up the digits, they always make 9, with the exception of 9+9:

1+8, 2+7, 3+6, 4+5, 9+0, 1+8

10 Times

The simplest to remember as all you have to do is take the number you are multiplying by and add a zero:

20 30 40 50 60 70 80 90 100 110 120

11 Times

This is fairly easy once you've noted that you just put two digits of the number you are multiplying by together:

11 x 2 = 22, 11 x 3 = 33, 11 x 4 = 44 and so on until:

11 x 10 – remember the 10x table and add a zero – 110

11 x 11 = 121

11 x 12 = 132

12 Times

If you have worked through all the tables, once you have reached 12 x you have already covered it and the only new number is:

$$12 \times 12 = 144$$

Working on the principle that the more connections you can make the more routes you have to remember, it's also useful to think that 12 is 10 x plus 2 x.

To help yourself further you can also draw out a multiplication square:

	1	2	3	4	5	6	7	8	9	10	11	12
1	1	2	3	4	5	6	7	8	9	10	11	12
2	2	4	6	8	10	12	14	16	18	20	22	24
3	3	6	9	12	15	18	21	24	27	30	33	36
4	4	8	12	16	20	24	28	32	36	40	44	48
5	5	10	15	20	25	30	35	40	45	50	55	60
6	6	12	18	24	30	36	42	48	54	60	66	72
7	7	14	21	28	35	42	49	56	63	70	77	84
8	8	16	24	32	40	48	56	64	72	80	88	96
9	9	18	27	36	45	54	63	72	81	90	99	108
10	10	20	30	40	50	60	70	80	90	100	110	120
11	11	22	33	44	55	66	77	88	99	110	121	132
12	12	24	36	48	60	72	84	96	108	120	132	144

This helps to fix the patterns in your mind and is a useful quick reference when needed!

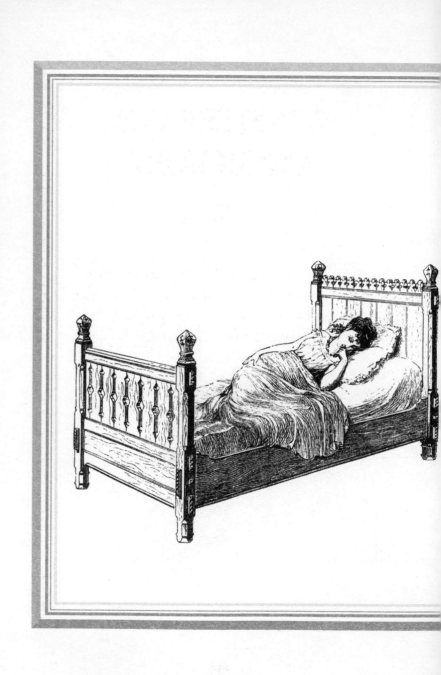

SLEEP
AND MEMORY

*'Early to bed and early to rise makes a man
healthy, wealthy and wise'.*

BENJAMIN FRANKLIN

Scientists now believe that sleep is essential for memory consolidation, the process by which a memory is coded and fixed so that it can be retrieved and used, for instance in an exam.

Several cleverly designed sleep deprivation experiments, including one at Harvard Medical School, have shown that if people did not sleep within 30 hours of studying, their memory of what they had tried to learn would be impaired. It appears that both Slow Wave and REM sleep, which occurs late in the sleep cycle, are necessary for the maximum improvement in performance and that there is a sequential process for memory consolidation at work. During REM sleep the brain and body become active, heart rate and blood pressure increase and there is characteristic eye shuddering, or rapid eye movements. Episodes last anything from 11 to 25 minutes and these are the periods of sleep which are most associated with dreaming. It is possible that the memories we don't think about are relived during REM sleep, in the form of dreams, so that we can recall them when needed.

Dr Andrew Tilley of the University of Queensland said, 'It looks like there's a window of opportunity following a learning episode in which sleep needs to occur in order for it to have beneficial effects on memory and that the window shuts around 26 to 30 hours.'

Further studies have also shown that sleep deprivation, particularly a lack of REM sleep, leads to poor performance in memory recall or logical tests and that memory loss occurs if a student is deprived of sleep on the two nights following a study session: this is particularly linked to the first and last two periods of REM sleep. Interestingly, REM density or the number of rapid eye movements per minute, have been found to increase for several nights after intense studying.

Not all scientists agree that there is a link between sleep and memory. Some argue that far from consolidating memories during REM episodes and dreams, the brain is actually using this time to dispose of unwanted material to avoid overload.

REVISING FOR EXAMS

*'To accomplish great things,
we must dream as well as act'*

ANATOLE FRANCE

It seems that granny might have been right when she advised a 'good night's sleep' and warned, 'If you don't know it by now you never will' when you were frantically cramming at the last minute for an exam.

BIOLOGY

'I've a grand memory for forgetting.'

ROBERT LOUIS STEVENSON

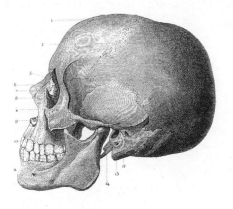

Scientists generally, but medical students in particular, have come up with the most incredible number of mnemonics for the names of bones and biochemical reactions. There are far too many to include here but the sheer volume and inventiveness is impressive. Here are just a few which may prove useful at some point.

TAXONOMIC CLASSIFICATIONS

Taxonomy is the science and practice of classification and in biological terms this refers to the hierarchical classification of organisms.

> *Kings Play Chess On Fridays Generally Speaking*, and
> *Katie Puts Cake On Fred's Good Shirt*,

are just two example of an old mnemonic for the division of animals into seven groups:

Kingdom, Phylum, Class, Order, Family, Genus, Species

Others include:

> *Kings Play Chess On Fine Green Silk.*

Kings Play Chess on Fine Grained Sand.
Kangaroos Pounce Cheekily On Fred's Green Sauce.
Kids Playing Catch On Freeways Go Splat.
Kryptonite Promotes Casualty Overwhelmingly For Great
  Superman.

And there are many, many others.

While zoologists use the word 'phylum' botanists substitute the term 'Division', so a better version for any botanist is:

King David Comes Over For Great Spaghetti.

There are also subdivisions within these groups and the complete Linnaean order of classification is:

Kingdom
  Subkingdom

Phylum
  Subphylum
  Superclass

Class
  Subclass
  Infraclass
  Cohort
  Superorder

Order
  Suborder
  Superfamily

Family
  Subfamily
  Tribe

Genus
  Subgenus

Species
  Subspecies

Man's Taxonomy

All Chaperones Must Previously Have Had Sex.

Animalia, Chordata, Mammalia, Primata, Hominidae, Homo, Sapiens.

THE SEVEN ACTIVITIES OF ALL LIVING THINGS

There are seven activities common to all living things in the cycle of life:

Movement,
Respiration,
Sensitivity,
Growth,
Reproduction,
Excretion,
Nutrition.

Generations of school children have been taught to remember them by the acronym:

MRS GREN

Or if you choose to call Sensitivity 'Excitability', you have:

MR GREEN

KREBS CYCLE

The Krebs Cycle was first recognised by the German bio-chemist, Hans Adolph Krebs in 1937. It is also known as the tri-carboxylic acid cycle (TCA) or citric acid cycle and refers to a complex series of chemical reactions in all cells which utilise oxygen in their respiration process. It is the metabolic pathway involved in the chemical conversion of carbohydrates, proteins and fats into carbon dioxide and water to generate usuable energy.

The eight stages are:

Citrate, Isocitrate, Ketoglutarate, Succinyl, Succinate, Fumarate, Malate, Oxaloacetate.

I have found two mnemonic sentences to remember them:

Can Intelligent Karen Solve Some Foreign Mafia Operations,

and

Cindy Is Kinky So She Fornicates More Often.

VERTEBRATE ANIMAL CLASSIFICATIONS

An easy way to remember the five classes is:

FARM B.

For: Fish, Amphibians, Reptiles, Mammals, Birds.

LICHEN

Lichen are made up of algae and fungi.

She was all gal (algae) and he was a fun guy (fungi).
They took a likin' (lichen) to each other . . .

SEDGES, RUSHES AND GRASSES

To tell which is which:

Sedges have edges
Rushes are round
Grasses are hollow right down to the ground.

And:
Sedges have edges,
Rushes are round,
And grasses like asses have holes.

THE BODY

The Human Skeleton

Tibia and Fibula

For the position, remember: the Fibula is lateral.
And

The Tibia is thick like a tuba,
The Fibula is thin like a flute.

Carpal Bones

The carpal bones are actually part of the wrist rather than the hand, allowing the joint to move and rotate. It is the bones of the metacarpus which are part of the hand.

Senior Lecturers Try Positions That They Can't Handle, or *Stop Letting Those People Touch That Cadaver's Hand*.

These give the eight carpal bones in order of position:

Scaphoid, Lunate, Triquetrum, Pisiform, Trapezium, Trapezoid, Capitate, Hamate.

Positions of the Trapezium and Trapezoid:

The Trapez**ium** is by the th**umb**, the Trapez**oid** is by its **side**.

The **H**amate has the **H**ook.

A rather more complicated version which gives more prompts for each bone is:

The Boat sailed to the Moon with Three PEAs in a rOw. At the wheel was Captain Hook.

Boat is Scaphoid,
Moon is Lunate,
Three is Triquetrum (also known as triquetral bone),
Peas is Pisiform,
Stress the EA sound in Peas for Trapezium,
Row is Trapezoid,

Captain is Capate (the largest of the bones and at the
     centre of the wrist),
Hook is Hamate.

Facial Bones

Virgil Cannot Make My Pet Zebra Laugh.

Vomer, Conchae, Nasal, Maxilla, Mandible, Palatine,
Zygomatic, Lacrimal.

Cranial or Skull Bones

Fraternity Parties Occasionally Teach Spartan Etiquette.

This gives the first two letters of each bone:

Frontal, Parietal, Occipital, Temporal, Sphenoid,
Ethmoid.

Or you may prefer: STEP OF(f my skull) or, PEST OF 6

The Bones of the Arm and Shoulder

*Some Crooks Have Underestimated Royal Canadian Mounted
Police.*

This gives the bones in order:

Scapula, Clavicle, Humerus, Ulna, Radius, Carpals,
Metacarpals, Phalanges.

The Leg Bones

Help Five Police To Find Ten Missing Prisoners.

In order:

Hip, Femur, Patella, Tibia, Fibula, Tarsals, Metarsals, Phalanges.

Vertebrae of the Spinal Column

Clever Dick Likes Sugar Candy.

Cervical, Dorsal (which is also known as Thoracic), Lumbar, Sacrum, Coccyx.

Ossification

Ossification is the normal process of bone formation. Initially, a child's skeleton is largely composed of relatively soft cartilage which gradually transforms into bones. Anatomists can remember the ages at which different bones harden:

Every Potential Anatomist Should Know When (bones ossify)
Elbow – 16 years
Pelvis – 17 years
Ankle – 17 years
Shoulder – 18 years
Knee – 18 years
Wrist – 19 years

The Inner Ear Bones

Describing the shape and position of the bones working inwards:

Take a Hammer — Malleus
Hit an Indian Elephant — Incus
Which puts its foot in a stirrup — Stapes

Another option is: **Ma**iling **Inc**ludes **St**amps.

THE 12 CRANIAL NERVES

There are twelve pairs of cranial nerves all with distinct functions.

Nerve	*Function*
I Olfactory	Smell
II Optic	Vision
III Oculomotor	Movement of eyelid and eyeball
IV Trochlear	Turns eye downward and laterally
V Trigeminal	Chewing, touch & pain in face & mouth
VI Abducens	Turns eye laterally

	Nerve	Function
VII	Facial	Controls most facial expressions, secretion of tears and saliva, taste
VIII	Auditory (or Vestibulocochlear)	Hearing and sense of equilibrium
IX	Glossopharyngeal	Taste, senses carotid blood pressure
X	Vagus	Senses aortic blood pressure, slows heart rate, stimulates digestive organs, taste
XI	Spinal Accessory	Swallowing movements, controls sternocleido-mastoid and trapezius
XII	Hypoglossal	Controls tongue movements

Medical students have devised a large number of mnemonics to help them remember these. One of the most used (and cleanest) is:

On Old Olympus' Towering Top, A Finn and German Viewed Some Hops.

And to remember whether a nerve is sensory (s), motor (m) or both (b), apply the first letter of the words of this twelve-word sentence to the correspondingly numbered nerve:

*Some Say Marry Money But My Brother Says
Big Boobs Matter More!*

WHITE BLOOD CELLS

Nobody Likes My Educational Background.

Which gives in order of decreasing numbers:

Neutrophils,
Lymphocytes,
Monocytes,
Eosinophils,
Basophils.

CELL CYCLE

Go Sally Go! Make Children!

G1, S, G2, M, C.

Or expressed more fully:

Growth phase 1, DNA Synthesis (replication),
Growth phase 2, Mitosis, Cytokinesis.

MITOSIS

People Meet And Talk, or

Prophase, Metaphase, Anaphase, Telophase.

For the five stages of cell division in Mitosis:

Interphase, Prophase, Metphase, Anaphase, Telophase,

I Painted My Attic Today.

EIGHT ESSENTIAL AMINO ACIDS

I Like To Teach My Vets Lumbar Puncture.

Isoleucine, Leucine, Threonine, Tryptophan, Methionine, Valine, Lysine, Phenylalanine.

ANIMALS

Elephants

What's the difference between an African and an Indian elephant?

It sounds like the beginning of a joke but there are a number of differences. The most obvious is that the African elephant is not only larger, but it also has bigger ears.

India's big and its elephant there features,
But Africa's bigger with much bigger creatures.

And:

India's big but Africa's bigger,
The same as their elephants — easy to figure.

Alongside the difference in ear size, there is also a difference in shape. As a rough guide, African elephants' ears usually resemble the outline of Africa with a definite extra curve at the top while Indian elephants' ears look more like the triangular shape of India.

ELEPHANT FACTS

· Both African and Indian elephants can smell water almost 5 km away.

· Elephants are the only mammals unable to jump. Although they have knees, they weigh too much.

· Elephants are strong swimmers.

· They can communicate over long distances through low-frequency sound which they pick up through the sensitive skin of their trunks and feet.

· Their gestation period is 22 months, the longest of any land animal and calves weigh about 113 kg.

· Prehistoric ancestors include hairy mammoths which may have survived until as recently as 2000 BC in their dwarf forms.

· Small prehistoric elephants the size of large pigs lived on the island of Crete during the Pleistocene epoch.

· They are a symbol of wisdom in Asia, where they are famed for their memory and intelligence.

· They have long been working animals, particularly in the logging industry in Asia, although it is usually females that are domesticated and tamed.

· War elephants were frequently used by armies in India, and later China and the Persian and Greek empires. They were famously taken across the Alps by Hannibal and a charging elephant could wreak havoc amongst infantry and cavalry soldiers.

- 'An elephant never forgets.' Elephants follow the same paths and seem to pass genetic memories of routes and places on through the generations. Each clan also has their own burial ground and they will help ailing members return there. They develop strong, lasting relationships with each other and indeed with humans

African elephants

- Both males and females have external tusks.
- They are generally less hairy than Indian (or Asian) elephants.
- African elephants have two 'fingers' at the tips of their trunks.
- There are two types of African elephant – Bush or Savannah and Forest – and recent evidence has suggested that they may be separate species, although this has yet to be universally accepted.
- Bush elephants are bigger. Males reach 4 metres at the shoulder and can weigh between 3,500 kg and a staggering 12,000 kg.
- Bush elephants are found in the savannah area south of the Sahara, ranging over grasslands, marshes and lake shores.
- The Forest elephant tends to be smaller and rounder, with thinner, straighter tusks.
- Forest elephants are found in the dense rainforests of Central and Africa, although they do overlap with Savannah territories.

· Male Forest elephants stand up to 3 metres tall at the shoulders and weigh up to 4,500 kg.

· For much of the 20th century, African elephant populations were in decline largely because of poaching.

· In 2007 it was estimated that there were between 470,000 and 690,000 elephants in the wild although the true figure is hard to determine. It does seem that the largest populations, found in Southern and Eastern Africa have been stable or steadily increasing since the 1990s.

· African elephants are faster and more powerful than their Indian cousins and far more difficult to train.

Indian or Asian elephants

· Only males have tusks; the females' are so small they are hardly visible.

· They have only one 'finger' at the tips of their trunks.

· Large males can be over 3 m tall and weigh up to 5,400 kg.

· White, or albino, elephants are considered sacred in Burma and Thailand.

· It is estimated that there are between 38,000 and 53,000 wild elephants and up to 15,300 domesticated elephants in Asia.

· Populations have declined but rather more gradually than those of African elephants, due mainly to poaching and loss of natural habitat.

Camels

There are two main species of camel: the Bactrian camel, which still exists in the wild in the colder regions of Central Asia, and the Arabian dromedary camel, which is lighter and faster, adapted to the dry desert areas of Western Asia and sub-Saharan Africa. Dromedaries were domesticated long ago and are extinct as a wild species.

To remember the obvious difference between the two:

A Bactrian camel has two humps like a B,
While a dromedary has one hump just like a D.

White and Black Rhinoceros

The names are confusing as they cannot really be distinguished by colour. 'White' was a mistranslation of a Dutch word 'weit' meaning wide.

To tell them apart, think white – wide, as the white rhino has a wide square snout while the black rhino has a tapering triangular snout.

CAMEL FACTS

· Roughly 90% of the world's 14 million camels, are dromedaries.

· There are an estimated 1.4 million Bactrian camels with around 1000 living wild in the Gobi Desert.

· Surprisingly there are up to 700,000 feral dromedaries in central Australia, thought to be descendants of escaped transport camels introduced by Afghans in the 19th and early 20th centuries.

· An adult stands about 1.85 m at the shoulders and 2.15 m to the top of the hump.

· Dromedary camels can reach speeds of 65 km per hour in short bursts with sustained speeds of 40 km/hour.

· Both dromedaries and bactrians are related to South American llamas, vicunas and alpacas.

· Fossils suggest camels evolved in North America during the Palaeogene period and later spread to Asia.

· Average life expectancy is 40 to 50 years.

· While it's said that elephants never forget, it's also claimed that camels never forget an injury.

RHINOCEROS FACTS

· Black rhinos are 140-170 cm tall at the shoulder and are up to 3.6 m in length. They typically weigh between 800 and 1364 kg, with the females smaller than the males.

· They have two horns made of keratin; the longest sits at

the front of the nose and is usually about 50cm, although they are occasionally much longer.

· Black rhinos' colour depends on the local soil and they are not usually actually black.

· There are four subspecies of black rhinoceros and in July 2006, the World Conservation Union declared the Western black rhino extinct with only a handful remaining in captivity.

· The black rhino's tapered, prehensile lip is used for grasping twigs and leaves while the white rhino's square snout is suited to eating grass.

· Both have very poor eyesight but excellent hearing and sense of smell. They have been known to charge tree trunks by mistake when they feel threatened.

· White rhinos are larger generally and also have larger ears and skulls, as well as a distinct hump on the neck.

· White rhinos are savannah-dwelling grazers; black rhinos live in forest and scrub. Black rhinos are classified as endangered; white as 'vulnerable'.

· Rhinoceros date from the Miocene epoch.

· White rhinos are more gregarious and both have an extensive 'vocabulary' of bellows, grunts, growls, squeaks and snort.

· In spite of its bulk, the rhinoceros is very agile and can reach speeds of up to 48 km per hour.

· They have a reputation for being bad tempered particularly in regions where they have been disturbed.

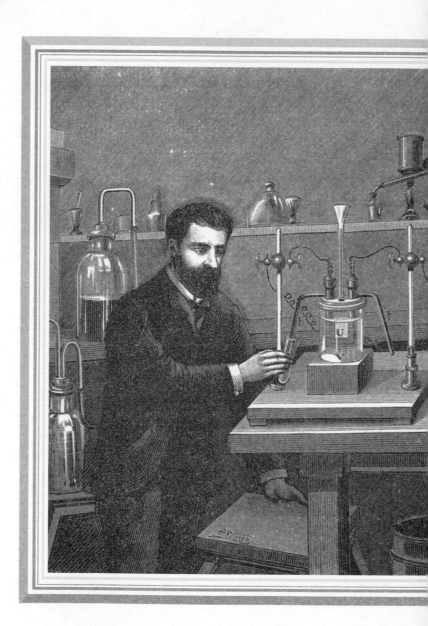

CHEMISTRY

'We are able to find everything in our memory which is like a dispensary or chemical laboratory in which chance steers our hand sometimes to a soothing drug and sometimes to a dangerous poison.'

Marcel Proust

Somehow I missed out on all but the most basic tuition in chemistry at school but I find that I now know parts of the periodic table of elements entirely thanks to Tom Lehrer's song. Written in the 1950s it is set to a version of Gilbert and Sullivan's 'I Am The Very Model of a Modern Major General', from 'The Pirates of Penzance'. Once you've heard it a few times, it tends to stick. If you're unfamiliar, you can find Lehrer's original plus various other versions on YouTube.

PERIODIC TABLE OF ELEMENTS

'There's antimony, arsenic, aluminium, selenium,
And hydrogen and oxygen and nitrogen and rhenium
And nickel, neodymium, neptunium, germanium,
And iron, americium, ruthenium, uranium,
Europium, zirconium, lutetium, vanadium
And lanthanum and osmium and astatine and radium
And gold, protactinium and indium and gallium
And iodine and thorium and thulium and thallium.

There's yttrium, ytterbium, actinium, rubidium
And boron, gadolinium, niobium, iridium,

And strontium and silicon and silver and samarium,
And bismuth, bromine, lithium, beryllium and barium.

There's holmium and helium and hafnium and erbium
And phosphorus and francium and fluorine and terbium
And manganese and mercury, molybdenum, magnesium,
Dysprosium and scandium and cerium and cesium
And lead, praseodymium, and platinum, plutonium,
Palladium, promethium, potassium, polonium,
Tantalum, technetium, titanium, tellurium,
And cadmium and calcium and chromium and curium.

There's sulphur, californium and fermium, berkelium
And also mendelevium, einsteinium and nobelium
And argon, krypton, neon, radon, xenon, zinc and rhodium
And chlorine, carbon, cobalt, copper,
Tungsten, tin and sodium.

These are the only ones of which the news has come to
    Harvard,
And there may be many others but they haven't been
    discovered.'

THE PERIODIC TABLE

The table is generally accredited to the Russian chemist Dmitri Mendeleev in 1869. It is designed to illustrate recurring or periodic trends in the properties of the elements. As new elements and theories explaining chemical behaviour have been developed, the table has been adapted and extended.

The elements are set in order of their atomic weights beginning with the lightest, which is hydrogen. It follows Mendeleev's Periodic Law stating, 'The properties of the elements are in periodic dependence upon their atomic weights.'

Since its invention, the Periodic Table has been widely used in all areas of science and engineering.

RARE GASES

Rare gases form Group O in the Periodic Table and are listed in order of atomic weight:

He – Helium, Ne – Neon, A – Argon, Kr – Krypton, Xe – Xenon, Rn – Radon.

These can be remembered by:

HEaven Never Asked KRiegspiel's Extra ReNt.

OXIDATION

To remind yourself that Oxidation is Loss and Reduction is Gain in the electron transfer chain, just think of:

OIL RIG

Or:

LEO the lion goes GER

Lose Electrons = Oxidation
Gain Electrons = Reduction

And:

ORE

Oxidation is Removal of Electrons.

MIXING ACIDS AND WATER

Add acid to water
Just as you oughta.

BIOCHEMICAL PATHWAYS

Aldohexoses which are monosaccharide sugars can be remembered by a mnemonic said to have been thought up by the chemist Emil Fisher:

All Atruists Gladly Make Gum in Gallon Tanks.

Allose, Altros, Glucose, Mannose, Gulose, Idose, Galactose, Tallose.

MEMORY TIPS OF A GRANDMASTER

Ed Cooke is a memory grandmaster. He has featured in the world memory championships top ten for the last six years and he is still only 26. He recently advised on how to learn verses in the national poetry recital competition for primary school children.

· He firmly believes that everyone is good at remembering something.

· The key is to be interested and motivated.

· And memory works best if you can make an emotional connection, which is one of the reasons why music can be so helpful as it immediately channels the emotional part of your brain.

· Think about how much you do remember. He points out that there is less information in a book, for example, than in your knowledge of what's in your home. Yet you don't even think about how you remember all that.

· When meeting someone, take an interest in them and repeat their name to yourself.

· We also remember the books we've read, the films we've watched and the CDs we have listened to.

• Don't underestimate your memory. He recalls, ' In an experiment they showed a group of people 1,800 photos and then tested them again after various lengths of time. Even 20 years later they were able to select a photo they had seen from one they hadn't. There is a colossal amount of information stored away.'

• When teaching children to learn poems, find ways to make the words as vivid as possible and provide landmarks in the structure.

• Use your imagination to create interest and an emotional response to what you are trying to memorise.

• Age doesn't have to limit your brain power. Keep your expectations of yourself high. Everyone's forgetful sometimes, it's not just old age.

PHYSICS

'Science may set limits to knowledge but should not set limits to imagination.'

Bertrand Russell

A knowledge of physics is fundamental to our understanding of the world and universe, and the laws which govern our existence. Included here are just a few of the more famous rules and theories.

EINSTEIN'S THEORY OF RELATIVITY AND THE SPEED OF LIGHT

Albert Einstein was one of the greatest physicists the world has known. His theory of relativity, put forward in the early part of the twentieth century is one of the most significant scientific advances . It recognises that the speed of light in a vacuum is constant. Which means that objects travelling close to the speed of light will appear to an observer on earth to move slower and shorten in length. The theory also gave rise to the famous equation:

$E = mc^2$

revealing the equivalence of mass and energy.

When applied to gravitational fields, the theory suggests the curve space-time continuum depicting the dimensions of space and time as a two-dimensional surface where large objects create dips in the surface.

The speed of light is always 299,792,458 metres per second which can be worked out by using the number of characters in a word to equal a digit:

As Einstein's equations validly predicted, we hold speed constant.

THE ELECTRO-MAGNETIC SPECTRUM

Cary Grant eXpects Unanimous Votes In Movie Reviews Tonight, helps to recall:

Cosmic, Gamma, X-rays, Ultraviolet, Visible, Infrared, Microwave, Radio, Television.

FLEMING'S RULE

Fleming's left-hand rule for electric motors shows the direction of the thrust on a conductor carrying a current in a magnetic field.

Hold the left hand with the thumb, index and middle fingers at right angles.

- The **Th**umb represents the direction of **Th**rust or Motion.
- The **F**irst finger represents the direction of the **F**ield.
- The se**C**ond finger represents the direction of the **C**urrent from positive to negative.

Fleming's right-hand rule for generators (or dynamos) shows

the direction of induced current flow when a conductor moves in a magnetic field.

Hold the right hand with the thumb, index and middle fingers at right angles.

- The Thu**M**b represents the direction of **M**otion of the conductor.
- The **F**irst finger represents the direction of the **F**ield.
- The se**C**ond of the induced or generated **C**urrent from positive to negative.

For both you can also use FBI as an acronym for:

Force which is the thumb,
B the magnetic field represented by the first finger,
I the direction of the current, represented by the second finger.

To remember whether to use the left or right hand:

M is for Mum and for Motors.
D is for Dad and for Dynamos.
Dad is always right.

OHM'S LAW

Discovered by Georg Ohm in 1827, the law shows the relationship between voltage (V), current in amps (A) and resistance (R). It can be expressed in three ways:

V = A x R,   A = V/R,   R = V/A

To remember these set out a triangle:

V

A   **R**

- To calculate Voltage V, cover the V. This leaves A R, so the equation is V = A x R.
- To calculate Current A, cover the A. This leaves V over R, so the equation is A = V/R.
- To calculate Resistence R, cover the R. This leaves V over A, so the equation is R = V/A.

RAINBOWS AND THE COLOUR SPECTRUM

The order of the seven colours of the light spectrum as seen so clearly in rainbows is:

Red, Orange, Yellow, Green, Blue, Indigo, Violet.

Scientists, especially Americans, often use:

ROY G. BIV

I have to say, I much prefer:

Richard Of York Gave Battle In Vain.

PRIMARY AND SECONDARY COLOURS

The primary colours of light are blue, green and red; when combined these three make total colour which is white light.

The secondary colours of yellow, magenta and cyan are used to make most other shades. They are also called subtractive colours as when they are combined they each absorb one primary colour of light so there is no light left to see.

The sentence used to remember this is:

Better Get Ready When
Your Mistress Comes Back.

Blue+Green+Red= White
Yellow+Magenta+Cyan= Black

FORCE AND MOTION

Distance, Speed and Velocity.

Distance is the measure of how far an object has travelled or far away it is. It is the same as length and is measured in metres.

Speed is a measure of how fast an object is travelling and is measured in metres per second.

Velocity also measures how fast an object is moving in metres per second, but it differs from speed in that velocity measures speed in one direction. If an object is moving in a straight line, speed and velocity are the same, but if it changes direction but remains at the same speed, velocity will have changed but speed remains the same.

To calculate speed, use the equation Speed = $\dfrac{\text{Distance}}{\text{Time}}$

This can be more easily remembered as an inverted triangle if it is written: AVERAGE SPEED

Equals

DISTANCE

Divided by

TIME

Likewise:

VELOCITY

Equals

DISTANCE

Divided by

TIME

NEWTON'S THREE LAWS OF MOTION

One: An object remains at rest or in uniform motion in a straight line unless an external force is applied to it.

This follows Galileo's concept of inertia and is often called 'The law of inertia'.

Two: An object's rate of change of momentum is proportional to the force causing it. The relationship between an object's mass 'm', its acceleration 'a' and the applied force F can be expressed as: $F = m \times a$. Or more simply summarised as acceleration is directly related to the force applied.

This is the most powerful of the three laws.

Three: For every action there is an equal and opposite reaction.

This law basically explains what happens if we step off a moving train onto the stationary platform.

As an aid to remembering them, think of the first as one (I) ertia, and the third as an upside down 3 which can be seen as 'equal and opposite'.

SIR ISAAC NEWTON

Isaac Newton was a physicist, mathematician, astronomer, theologian, alchemist and natural philosopher, and the greatest scientist of his age. He was born on 4 January 1643 in Woolsthorpe, Lincolnshire. It was at Cambridge University that he became interested in mathematics, physics, astronomy and optics but the plague forced the university to close in October 1665 and he returned home. He later described the two years 1665 and 1666, as the 'prime of my age for invention'. It was at this time that he began to think about gravity and to develop his idea on calculus.

In 1667, Newton returned to Cambridge where he became a fellow of Trinity College and was later appointed second Lucasian Professor of Mathematics.From the mid-1660s Newton conducted experiments on the composition of light, discovering that white light is composed of the same colours as the rainbow. It was this work particularly after the development of his reflecting telescope in 1668 that captured the attention of the scientific world and he was made a Fellow of the Royal Society in 1672. In 1704 he published *The Opticks* which outlined his discoveries on light and colour and established the modern study of the behaviour of light.

Newton published widely, his most famous single work being the *Philosophia Naturalis Principia Mathematica* (Mathematical Principles of Natural Philosophy) published in 1687 with the help of the astronomer Edmond Halley. In it he described universal gravitation, how a universal force such as gravity applied to all objects in all parts of the universe as well as the three laws of motion. He demonstrated the consistency between Kepler's laws of planetary motion and his theory of gravity. His findings removed the last doubts about heliocentrism and advanced the scientific revolution. These principles were to dominate the scientific view of the universe for the next three centuries.

In 1689 Newton became MP for Cambridge University and was appointed warden of the Royal Mint in 1696. He was knighted in 1705 and elected president of the Royal Society, an office he held until his death in 1727. He is buried in Westminster Abbey.

PHYSICS

COLOUR BANDS ON RESISTORS

There are several versions of mnemonic sentences to help remember the colour codes of resistors, capacitors and other electronic components. Most are very un-PC. Here are two more acceptable examples:

Billy Brown Revives On Your Gin But Values Good Whisky.

Black, Brown, Red, Orange, Yellow, Green, Blue, Violet, Grey, White, and if you want to add Gold or Silver tolerance:

Betty Brown Races Over Your Gran But Violet Generally Wins Gold or Silver.

ASTRONOMY

*'Astronomy compels the soul to look upwards
and leads us from this world to another.'*

PLATO

L ike many people, I had the order of the planets in the solar system fixed firmly in my mind through the mnemonic 'My Very Educated Mother Just Served Us Nine Pies,' along with a suitable revision when Pluto was demoted. However, until I began researching this book I had no idea how many alternative versions of the mnemonic there were, nor just how many others existed for anything to do with the stars and planets.

THE PLANETS OF THE SOLAR SYSTEM

There are many versions of mnemonic sentences to place the planets in the correct order in the Solar System. Working out from the sun at the centre they are:

Mercury, Venus, Earth, Mars, Jupiter, Saturn, Uranus, Neptune, Pluto.

My preferred one is:

My Very Educated Mother Just Served Us Nine Pies.

Of course, you also need to remember that every 248 years Neptune becomes the furthest planet for 20 years, in which case you could end the sentence with 'Pine Nuts'. This last happened between 1979 and 2000.

And if you want them in reverse:

Plainly, Naughty Uncensored Sex Jokes Make Embarrassed Virgins Mad.

PLANETS IN ORDER OF SIZE

The planets of the Solar System in order of mass and equatorial diameter are, largest first:

Jupiter, Saturn, Uranus, Neptune, Earth, Venus, Mars, Mercury, Pluto.

Which can be remembered as:

Jason Sat Under Ninety Eight Vicious Monster Munching Penguins.

And in ascending order, smallest first:

Pluto Must Meet Venus Every Night Until Saturn Jumps, or *Pop Music Makes Vikings Even Naughtier Until Saxons Jiggle.*

And to distinguish Mars from Mercury:

Pluto's Mercenaries March Valiantly Every Night Up Satan's Jockstrap.

Of course, all of these were devised before the debate over whether or not Pluto is a planet.

Pluto is not a planet . . .

There has also been considerable debate over whether Pluto can really be classified as a planet at all. In August 2006, the International Astronomical Union ruled that the distant ice-covered world is a large example of a collection of objects called the Kuiper Belt. It has been reclassified as a dwarf planet: just one of more than 40 discovered so far, including the large asteroid Ceres and a very distant object nicknamed Xena, discovered in 2007 by the astronomer Mike Brown of the California Institute at Pasadena.

Correcting the mnemonic after the demotion of Pluto:

My Very Educated Mother Just Served Us Noodles.

And if you want to include the Milky Way Galaxy:

My Very Educated Mother Just Served Us Nuts Mixed With Grapes.

However, that's not the end of the story. Under a planet definition supported by Mark Sykes, Director of the Planetary Science Institute, if an object is massive enough to be round and orbit a star, then it should be classified as a planet.

This means that Pluto would be reinstated and would also add:

Ceres – now identified as the smallest dwarf planet, formerly the first and largest asteroid to be discovered. It was found by Guisseppe Piazzi in 1801 and orbits between Mars and Jupiter. Ceres may have an ocean of liquid water beneath the surface, making life a possibility;

Charon – now a dwarf planet, but formerly the largest of Pluto's moons;

Makemake – officially named in July 2008, previously nicknamed 'Xena', Makemake orbits beyond Pluto;

Eris – discovered in January 2005, by a Palomar Observatory-based team led by Mike Brown, Eris is the largest dwarf planet;

Haumea – named after a Hawaiian goddess, the dwarf planet nicknamed 'Santa', was officially named in September 2008.

This would make the order of the official planets and minor planets of the solar system:

Mercury,
Venus,
Earth,
Mars,
Ceres,
Jupiter,
Saturn,
Uranus,
Neptune,
Pluto,
Eris,
Makemake,
Haumea.

And the mnemonic:

> *My Very Exciting Moment Cementing Justice, Sweetly Usurped Naughty People Cleverly Evading Mainstream Honour.*

THE MOONS OF JUPITER

Amalthea, Io, Europa, Ganymede, Callisto.

> *An Icecube Ever Grows Colder.*

And if we leave out Amalthea and concentrate on the four major Galilean moons:

> *Il Est Grand, Charles.*

Jupiter's Moons

Galileo Galilei first discovered Jupiter's four major moons in 1610 using a 20-power telescope; of the four, Ganymede is the largest, followed by Callisto. Further moons were discovered from the end of the 19th century and there are now 63 others known to astronomers, with probably more as yet unfound. All have been given the names of daughters, lovers and conquests of the Roman god Jupiter or his Greek equivalent, Zeus.

NEPTUNE'S MOON

Naiad, Thalasso, Despina, Galatea, Larissa, Proteus, Triton, Nereid:

Neptune's Tiny Dancing Girls Look Pretty Tonight.

Neptune has 13 moons as well as rings probably made of rocks and dust, unlike Saturn's bright rings made of ice.

The largest is Triton, discovered in 1846 by the English astronomer, William Lassell just days after Neptune itself was sighted by a Berlin observatory. Triton is ice-covered, with geysers shooting ice 8km into the thin atmosphere. Its surface reflects back so much of the little sunlight that reaches it that it is one of the coldest objects in the Solar System with temperatures around -240° C. There may be water beneath the ice making some form of life possible and the moon's centre is almost certainly geologically active.

Neptune's other moons are far smaller. Nereid was discovered in 1949, while Naiad, Thalasso, Despina, Galatea, Larissa and Proteus were located by Voyager 2 in 1989. As Neptune was the Roman god of the sea its moons are named after Roman and Greek nymphs and sea gods. Five more small moons were found between 2002 and 2003, none of which have so far been officially named.

SATURN'S MOONS

Mimas, Enceladus, Tethys, Dione, Rhea, Titan, Hyperion, Iapetus, Phoebe.

Which form the acronym:

MET DR THIP

Although 'Thip' is an unlikely name, this is oddly unforgettable.

Saturn's nine moons were all discovered before 1900: the largest, Titan, was found in 1655 by Christian Huygens, then Tethys, Dione, Rhea and Iapetus between 1671 and 1684 by Giovani Domenico Cassini, Mimas and Enceladus in 1789 by William Herschel and Hyperion by W. C. Bond, G. P. Bond and William Lassell. All were discovered using optical telescopes. With the invention of long-exposure photographic plates it became possible to discover further moons and Phoebe was found in 1899 by W. H. Pickering.

Saturn is now known to have 61 moons with confirmed orbits, 53 of which have names. The 38 smaller irregular satellites whose orbits are farther from Saturn are classified into groups with names from Gallic, Norse and Inuit mythologies. The 23 regular satellites have traditionally been given the names of Titans or other mythological figures associated with Saturn.

Saturn Facts

· Saturn is the second largest planet in the solar system (Jupiter is the largest).

· At its equator, Saturn's diameter is 74,600 miles, almost 10 times the diameter of the Earth.

· It was named after the Roman god of agriculture.

· Although the planet can be seen from Earth without a telescope its seven rings cannot.

· Saturn has a solid inner core but its surface is gas.

· Its atmosphere is mainly hydrogen and helium.

· It has the lowest density of all the planets and is so light it would float if there was an ocean large enough.

· An object weighing 100 pounds on Earth would weigh 116 pounds on Saturn.

· It takes over 29 years for Saturn to orbit the sun.

· Titan is the only one of Saturn's moons to have an atmosphere.

· Titan is actually larger than the planet Mercury.

· Titan's atmosphere is so dense that it is only recently that astronomers have begun to see its surface. They have discovered lakes of liquid methane and ethane near the poles and clouds in the atmosphere.

· Recent images from the Cassini spacecraft suggest that Titan has geological features which are similar to Earth's.

· A giant crater on the surface of Mimas makes it resemble the 'Death Star' in *Star Wars*.

- Iapetus is dark on one side and very bright on the other.
- Pandora and Prometheus are dubbed the shepherd moons because they herd particles into Saturn's 'F' ring.
- Phoebe is extremely dark, with an unusual orbit which leads astronomers to think is may be an asteroid or object from the Kuiper Belt which was caught by Saturn's strong gravitational pull aeons ago.

Enceladus

In June 2009 scientists reported that Enceladus, a tiny moon of Saturn could be one of the most promising places in the Solar System to search for extraterrestrial life.

A probe from Nasa's Cassini spacecraft has detected ice crystals of sodium salts which seem to come from plumes emanating from the south pole. These are similar to those found in our own oceans and support scientists' belief that there may be liquid water in caverns beneath the icy surface of Enceladus.

'We need three ingredients for life, as far as we know – liquid water, energy and the basic chemical building blocks – and we seem to have all three at Enceladus,' said John Spencer, a Cassini scientist from Southwest Research Institute, Boulder, Colorado.

THE MOON

Have you ever looked at a sliver of silver moon and wondered whether it was waxing or waning? Just think:

When **C**oming the moon is really departing.
When **D**eparting it is really coming.

Or put another way:

A l**E**ft-hand curve to the crescent means the moon is waning or d**E**creasing.
A r**I**ght-hand curve to the crescent means it is waxing or **I**ncreasing.

And:

DOC

D = Waxing.
O = Full.
C = Waning, so when the moon's coming it's actually going.

STELLAR CLASSIFICATION

The ordered system for classifying stars was originally developed by Annie Jump Cannon, 1863-1941. It is sometimes also called a 'temperature sequence' as it links the spectrum of each star to its surface temperature.

Starting with the hottest, stars are classified in descending order as:

The expression 'once in a blue moon' comes about because, not surprisingly, blue moons are rare – well, they happen once every two and a half years. Blue moons are not blue, it just means there have been two full moons in the same calendar month.

A harvest moon refers to the full moon closest to the autumn equinox when the moon rises for several nights at about the same time as sunset. They were beloved by farmers as they gave precious extra light at harvest time enabling farmers to carry on working after the sun went down.

A hunter's moon is the first full moon after harvest moon, which coincided with the start of the hunting season.

O, B, A, F, G, K, M.

Which has led to the very well-known astronomical mnemonic:

Oh Be A Fine Girl, Kiss Me.

Or sometimes:

Only Boys Advocating Feminism Get Kissed Meaningfully.

Our Sun is a class G in this spectral class system and depending on their size and composition, stars can also be classified as:

R, N, S (which can be added to the first mnemonic as: *Right Now Sweetie*), C, L, T.

Which can be remembered as:

Research Needs Support. Clever Loving's Tender.

The classifications R, N, S, and C are given to stars with high carbon content; L and T to stars that are so small they do not generate enough heat to begin nuclear fusion.

REMEMBERING NAMES AND FACES

'I cannot tell what the dickens his name is.'

WILLIAM SHAKESPEARE,
The Merry Wives of Windsor

Many people confess they are terrible at remembering names and faces. In actual fact, they remember the face perfectly well and quite possibly where they met the person, it's the name that eludes them.

Facial recognition is a key part of human perception. The youngest newborn baby quickly learns to recognise its mother's face and soon adds those of other relations and close family friends to this memory store. There have been a number of scientific studies in which groups were shown photographs of faces and other objects and then tested to see what they remembered, hours and days later. In all cases, faces were always by far the most easily recalled.

It seems such a natural thing to do to recognise a face, but think about it for a moment. Most of us recognise thousands of faces: there are the faces of people we know well and those of acquaintances but we add to these all those people we just see regularly or even occasionally. There are faces we recognise from the train or bus, from college, work, the bank, the super-market, all people we have maybe never even spoken to, but we know their face. Then there are actors, film stars, news-readers, presenters, celebrities whose faces appear on television, in magazines and newspapers. We recognise and remember them all even after a gap of years and usually know their names too, depending on how interested we are. We also recognise their different expressions and fairly successfully work out what these mean.

Recognising faces and expressions is a cognitively complex task. First the brain has to identify a face, next whether it is familiar or not, and finally interpret the expression, encoded in the arrangement of eyes and mouth. In the 1990s, scientists narrowed the brain's ability to recognise faces to a region called the fusiform face area, or FFA, located near the back of the brain on the bottom surface, within the fusiform gyrus in the temporal lobe. Magnetic Resonance Imaging shows this is in a slightly different position for each person and suggests there is also a 'place processor' close to the 'face processor'.

A number of experiments are ongoing to reveal exactly how our brain recognises and perceives faces. Interestingly, scientists have found that if photographs of famous faces are turned upside down, most people have difficulty recognising them. In one study, the eyes and eyebrows were inverted: when the pictures were the right way up everyone spotted the mistake instantly, not surprisingly, it looked extremely odd, but in the upside-down photos, the error was not obvious at all. However, the ability of face-blind people to recognise faces actually improves if the faces are upside down. Face blindness, or prosopagnosia, is the inability to recognise faces and can be inherited in rare cases, or the result of an injury or disease affecting the face recognition region of the brain.

If recognising faces is not the problem, how do we improve

our ability to remember names and more importantly, match the right name to the face? A person's name is important to them. We are all programmed to react to our own name. How many times have you looked up when you heard your name called, even when you knew it was not you who was being addressed? It's a natural response. So it follows that by using someone's name you will immediately please them and make them feel important. One of the problems is that names usually have no connection to faces. In the past this was often not the case and surnames at least tended to be associated with professions or jobs like Thatcher or Cooper, or a physical feature such as Redhead. Creating an association or connection for yourself is just one of the practical steps you can take to improve your memory for names.

TEN TIPS FOR REMEMBERING NAMES AND FACES

Be interested. Make a conscious decision to take your time when introduced to someone for the first time.

Listen to their name. This sounds obvious but often we are so caught up in what we are going to say that we don't really hear the name in the first place and it's not surprising that we can't remember it later.

Repeat the name immediately. You can do this quite casually to verify that you heard the name correctly, or to check whether the person prefers a shortened or lengthened version of their name. Repeat the name to yourself and again aloud on parting. If you're meeting several people at the same time, there's no shame in requesting a repetition immediately to make sure you know who's who.

Repetition is particularly important if it's an unfamiliar name and in that case it's worth repeating it several times in your head, breaking it into syllables and really exaggerating the sounds to fix them in your memory.

Really look at the person's face. We know our brains are good at remembering faces, so mentally reconstruct their face in your mind making a note of any unusual or distinctive feature; it could be something you particularly like or even dislike. Create a cartoon version but make sure you can hear the person's name as you picture it. You can also add any other non-visual features that stand out such as a strong accent.

Face association. If you know another person, or someone famous, with the same name, picture that person's face alongside this new person. Forge a connection.

Make a mind picture of the name. Turn the name into a picture. It could be something simple like a person 'bobbing' up and down behind a wall for Bob, or an image for the whole name. For instance, Sandra Rowe could become an egg timer filled with sand with little arms frantically rowing a boat across a choppy lake. The more colourful or bizarre the image, the more likely it is to stick.

Imagine writing the name, in different scripts and colours, saying it aloud to yourself as you write. Really visualise the name and ask to clarify the spelling if it is at all unusual. People won't mind, it shows you are really interested.

Franklin D. Roosevelt seemed to remember the names of virtually everyone he met effortlessly. Apparently he used to imagine the person's name written across their forehead. You could develop this by changing the calligraphy or design depending upon the sort of person they are: the name could be engraved in wood, jewelled, plain, colourful or even embroidered on an appropriate hat. Paris Hilton could wear a jewelled tiara of her name, someone called Alice could wear an Alice band or, if you prefer rhymes, a palace-shaped hat. The possibilities are endless, just use your imagination and have fun.

Exchange cards, especially in a business setting. The Japanese consider card exchange a major social function, just as the Victorians and Edwardians used to leave calling cards. If you've met someone in an official capacity, write down their name and where you met them in a notebook or computer file for future reference when needed.

Trust yourself. Stop making excuses or telling yourself you are dreadful at remembering names and instead just concentrate.

GEOGRAPHY

*Many complain of their memory,
few of their judgment.*

BENJAMIN FRANKLIN

G eographical mnemonics such as the ones for stalagmites and -tites, latitude and longitude, the tropics, great lakes and oceans were all long ago firmly fixed in my memory. Others, like the song 'Fifty Nifty United States', were a real revelation and they obviously work: I found a clip of a four-year-old girl who could sing her way through the states perfectly although she could barely pronounce some of the names.

OCEANS

The four oceans of the world, Indian, Arctic, Atlantic and Pacific can be remembered by:

I Am A Person.

THE SEVEN CONTINENTS

Eat An Aspirin After A Nighttime Snack, or
SEAN got three AAAs!

are mnemonics for the seven continents. The second letter in the first three A words helps to recall the A continents:

Europe, Antarctica, Asia, Africa, Australia, North
America, South America.

In order of size, beginning with the smallest, they are:

Australia
Europe
Antarctica
South America
North America
Africa
Asia

Audrey Excites Another Sailor. Nothing Affects Alistair.

COMPASS POINTS

To remember directions, use the sentence:

Never Eat Shredded Wheat, or
Never Eat Soggy Wafers.

Think of a clock face and place the first letter of each word
under the 12, 3, 6 and 9 beginning with N at 12 o'clock.

LONGITUDE AND LATITUDE

LONGitude is the distance ALONG the Equator starting from
0° at Greenwich or the Prime Meridian in London.

LATitude is the lateral or sideways distance in degrees

north or south from the Equator which is zero degrees latitude.

It also helps to think of longitude as long which always sounds vertical or tall.

THE EQUATOR AND THE TROPICS

CaNcer lies North of the Equator
And CapricOrn lies Opposite or South.

More simply, just remember cancer tends to affect the chest and corns are found on feet, so Capricorn lies below Cancer.

The equator is the longest line of latitude at 40,075.16 km long and it divides the Earth into the northern and southern hemispheres. The sun is directly overhead on the equator at noon on the two equinoxes around 21 March and September. It runs through Indonesia, Ecuador, Brazil, the Democratic Republic of the Congo and Kenya.

The tropics of Cancer and Capricorn mark the lines where the sun is directly overhead at noon on the two solstices: the tropic of Cancer on 21 June marking the beginning of summer in the northern hemisphere and winter in the southern; and the tropic of Capricorn on 21 December marking the start of summer in the southern hemisphere and winter in the northern.

The tropic of Cancer lies at 23.5° latitude north of the equator. Beginning at the Greenwich or Prime Meridian at zero degrees longitude heading eastwards, the tropic of

Cancer runs through: Algeria, Niger, Libya, Egypt, the Red Sea, Saudi Arabia, United Arab Emirates, Oman, the Indian Ocean, India, Bangladesh, Burma, China, the Taiwan Strait, the Republic of China, the Pacific Ocean, Hawaii (the sea area only), Mexico, Gulfs of California, Mexico, and Straits of Florida, the Bahamas, Atlantic Ocean, Western Sahara, Mauritania, Mali, Algeria.

The tropic of Capricorn lies at 23.5° latitude south of the equator and runs through Australia, Chile, southern Brazil (which is the only country which is crossed by both the equator and a tropic), Namibia, Madagascar and Mozambique. Beginning at zero degrees longitude and moving eastward, the tropic of Capricorn passes through: the Atlantic Ocean, Namibia, Botswana, South Africa, Mozambique, the Indian Ocean, Madagascar, the Indian Ocean, Australia, the Pacific Ocean, Chile, Argentina, Paraguay, Brazil, the Atlantic Ocean. The positions of both tropics are not actually fixed but can vary over time depending on the tilt of the Earth's axis relative to the plane of its orbit around the sun. Latitudes above the tropic of Cancer are known as the northern temperate zone and south of the tropic of Capricorn as the southern temperate zone.

THE WORLD'S LONGEST RIVERS

There can be differences of opinion on this according to the determination of the river's course and its tributaries, but this acronym is still useful:

NAMMI YACH-Y

Nile (Africa) 6,670 km
Amazon (South America) 6,400 km, although the largest by volume
Mississippi and Missouri, as a combined river system (USA)
Irtysh (Russia)
Yangtse (China)
Amur (Asia)
Congo (Africa)
Huang-Ho, or Yellow (China)

NORTH AFRICA

The countries of North Africa from west to east are:

Morocco, Algeria, Tunisia, Libya, Egypt.

Many African Tourists Like Elephants, is a neat reminder.

AMERICA

North America

The Fifty States

To remember the number of states, think of the song title by Ray Charles: 'Fifty Nifty United States' which, if you know the lyrics too, lists each by name. To hear the whole song, simply go to YouTube and pick your preferred version.

Here are the words:

Fifty Nifty United States from thirteen original colonies;
Fifty Nifty stars on the flag that billows so beautifully in the breeze.
Each individual state contributes a quality that is great.
Each individual state deserves a bow, we salute them now.

Fifty Nifty United States from thirteen original colonies,
Shout 'em, scout 'em, tell all about 'em,
One by one, till we've given a day to every state in the USA.
Alabama, Alaska, Arizona, Arkansas, California, Colorado, Connecticut,
Delaware, Florida, Georgia, Hawaii, Idaho, Illinois, Indiana.
Iowa, Kansas, Kentucky, Louisiana, Maine,
Maryland, Massachusetts, Michigan,
Minnesota, Mississippi, Missouri, Montana,
Nebraska, Nevada.
New Hampshire, New Jersey, New Mexico, New York,
North Carolina, North Dakota, Ohio,

Oklahoma, Oregon, Pennsylvania, Rhode Island, South
Carolina,
South Dakota, Tennessee, Texas,
Utah, Vermont, Virginia, Washington, West Virginia,
Wisconsin, Wyoming.

North, South, East, West in a calm, objective opinion (*choose
your favourite State*)
Is the Best of the Fifty Nifty United States from thirteen
original colonies
Shout 'em, scout 'em, tell all about 'em
One by One, till we've given a day to every state in the good
old U . . . S . . . A.

I was surprised by quite how much there is in the same vein,
so if the idea appeals, check out Animaniacs' video of Wakko's
50 State Capitals and Presidents; and also Yakko's Nations of
the World and Universe Song, to name just a few.

And, working on the principle that it's far easier to remember which state you have forgotten if you at least know what
letter it begins with, this nonsense sentence is helpful – just
ignore all the 'Es' and remember not to add a 'b' to numb!

*Evening Arctic snow can num mammoth Mike's lip, knee
and even me. Few ewe mow me.*

211

The States Next to California

To be sure which states border California:

On top	is Oregon
Next to	Nevada
Also next to	Arizona
Much down	Mexico
Precisely west	Pacific Ocean

The Great Lakes

The Great Lakes Huron, Ontario, Michigan, Erie and Superior can be easily remembered as the first letter of each spells:

HOMES.

Sam's Horse Must Eat Oats, recalls them in order of size, and to geographically place them from west to east:

Sally Made Henry Eat Oreos.

CENTRAL AMERICA

The countries of Central America from north to south are:

Mexico, Belize, Guatemala, El Salvador, Honduras, Nicaragua, Costa Rica, Panama, which can be more easily brought to mind by:

My Goodness But Eating Hot Nachos Causes Pain.

Alternately, you could exclude Mexico and remind yourself of

the Central American countries south of the border in several
sentences:

Beatrice, Give Every Hungry Nerd Cocoa Puffs.
Big Gorillas Eat Hotdogs Not Cold Pizza.
Big Grandmother Earned Her Nickels Cooking Pies.
Big George Earned His Noodles Causing Pain.

LAND BIOMES

Biomes are the world's major habitats. They are specialised
ecosystems defined by their environment: factors like
temperature, rainfall, altitude and latitude and by the animals
and vegetation found there.

There are six major land biomes:

Tundras,
Deciduous forests,
Deserts,
Grasslands,
Tropical rain forests,
Coniferous forests.

They can be remember by:

The Dry Desert Grows Terrific Castles.

STALACTITES AND STALAGMITES

There are several mnemonics to distinguish between the two:

*Stala**c**tites point from **c**eiling downwards, and
Stala**g**mites point **g**round upwards.*

Or:

*Stala**ctites** **c**ling **tight**,
Stala**gmites** grow **mighty**.*

I have to say I find it easier to just think,

Tights fall down, while mites crawl on the ground.

Stalactites and stalagmites form in pairs in limestone caves, due to water dripping and evaporating, leaving behind deposits of calcium carbonate dissolved from rock which build up over thousands of years. Stalactites tend to be long and thin, looking something like icicles. Stalagmites form directly below as the water falls to the floor and the resulting splash means they are usually shorter and thicker than stalactites. Eventually the two meet to form a single column.

GEOLOGICAL TIME PERIODS

Ever wondered which came first, the Jurassic or the Cretaceous or when exactly the Cambrian was? Just remember:

Pregnant Camels Often Sit Down Carefully. Perhaps Their Joints Creak?

This should help you get the correct order for each Period: Pre-Cambrian, Ordovician, Silurian, Devonian, Carboniferous, Permian, Triassic, Jurassic, Cretaceous.

To add the more recent epochs to these, remember:

Possibly Early Oiling Might Prevent Painful Rheumatism.

Paleocene, Eocene, Oligocene, Miocene, Pliocene, Pleistocene, Recent.

Or you could use:

Possibly Early Oiling Might Prevent Premature Hollowing,

if you prefer to include Holocene rather than Recent.

Periods & Epochs	Million years ago	Key events
Pre-Cambrian	up to 544	Land masses begin to break up, algae and trace fossils.
Cambrian	500-440	Major diversification in the Cambrian Explosion. First green plants and fungi.
Silurian	440-410	First millipedes and jawed fishes, corals, trilobites and molluscs.
Devonian	410-360	Large primitive trees, early form of sharks.
Carboniferous	360-286	Appearance of winged insects, amphibians, first reptiles and coal forests.
Permian	286-245	Permian Triassic extinction event destroying 95% of

Periods & Epochs	Million years ago	Key events
		life including trilobites. Mosses and seed plants, beetles and flies appear.
Triassic	245-208	Dinosaurs dominant on land and sea. Early mammals and primitive crocodiles.
Jurassic	208-146	Conifers and ferns widespread. First birds and lizards appear along with many dinosaurs including sauropods, carnosaurs and stegosaurs.
Cretaceous	146-65	Appearance of mammals, flowering plants, new types of insects, ammonites, new types of

Periods & Epochs	Million years ago	Key events
		dinosaurs including tyrannosaurs, modern sharks and crocodiles.
Tertiary Period	65 -1.8	
Paleocene	65-54	Tropical climate. Mammals diversify and first large mammals appear following the extinction of the dinosaurs.
Eocene	54-37	Lowering of CO_2 levels.
Oligocene	38-23	Rapid evolution and diversification of flora and fauna.
Miocene	23-1.8	Recognisable mammal and bird families. First apes, grasses and forests.
Quaternary Period	1.8 – today	

Periods & Epochs	Million years ago	Key events
Pleistocene	1.8 – 11,000	Humans appear.
Recent	11,000 – today	Development of human culture, beginning of global warming and climate change.

MOHS HARDNESS SCALE

The Mohs Scale of mineral hardness groups minerals into ten groups in ascending order according to their relative hardness. It was created by the German mineralogist Friedrich Mohs in 1812 and assesses the scratch-resistance of various minerals. This is just one method of defining hardness but the basic idea seems to have its roots in antiquity mentioned by Theophrastus around 300 BC and Pliny the Elder in *Naturalis Historia* around 77 BC.

The minerals in each group are capable of scratching those in the preceding group.

The Mohs Scale

1	Talc or mica	Used in talcum powder.
2	Gypsum or rock salt	Formed when seawater evaporates. Used in plaster of Paris.
3	Calcite	Limestone and many shells contain calcite.
4	Fluorite	Fluorine to prevent tooth decay is found in fluorite.
5	Apatite	A group of phosphate minerals. Hydroxylapatite is the major component of tooth enamel.
6	Orthaclase	Also known as feldspar, the most abundant mineral in the Earth's continental crust.
7	Quartz	Second most abundant mineral after feldspar.
8	Topaz	Pure topaz is colourless and transparent but it is usually tinted with impurities.
9	Corundum	Rubies and sapphires are corundums. Twice as hard as topaz.
10	Diamond	Prized in jewellery, also used in cutting tools. Four times as hard as corundum.

Groups 1 and 2 can be scratched by a fingernail, 3 to 6 by a knife, and groups 7-10 are hard enough to scratch glass. There are also some everyday items which can fit into the scale:

A fingernail is 2.5, a knife blade and glass are 5.5, and a steel file 6.5.

There are several mnemonic sentences to remember each group:

Toronto Girls Can Flirt And Only Quit To Chase Dwarves.

Terrible Giants Can Find Alligators Or Quaint Tigers Conveniently Digestible.

True Geologists Climb Faults And Observe Quarries To Contemplate Deformation.

HOW DO ACTORS LEARN LINES?

*'Learning is not attained by chance,
it must be sought for with ardour and attended
to with diligence.'*

Abigail Adams

223

To most outside the theatrical profession, learning lines seems one of the most difficult tasks facing an actor, involving endless hours spent poring over their part in an effort to memorise their the script. In fact that is not the way most actors work, and it is certainly not the most effective way to learn.

In a Columbia University discussion on memory, Michael Boyd, the artistic director of the Royal Shakespeare Company, and Oliver Sacks, professor of neurology and psychiatry at Columbia University Medical Center, looked at the idea of learning lines and memory being more than just a mental process. Michael Boyd, the artistic director of the RSC, worked with some thirty actors over a period of three years on the RSC's last complete cycle of Shakespeare's history plays. All of the actors were involved in at least seven plays, with a vast number of roles and lines to learn. Several of the plays were not worked on at all for almost a year, and when they returned to them, all the actors were very concerned that they would have forgotten their lines. And indeed it seemed they had. Working alone and during a line-run recall was generally poor. It wasn't until they stood on stage and began acting, even without costumes, props and scenery, that the actors remembered their parts. In fact, they remembered so well they were almost immediately word perfect. They were even better when there was an audience.

It seemed the memory of the lines was still there but it needed unlocking by a combination of body movement and, most importantly, emotion. Increasingly evidence suggests that memory is not just a mental process but something that involves the whole body. Michael Boyd went on to cite a neurobiological study of London taxi drivers that showed their hippocampi (the parts of their brain involved in memory) were enlarged after they had taken the test known as 'the-knowledge'. More relevant to his work with actors though, taxi drivers only remembered locations if they physicalised their memory: their sense of location was dependent upon them having a physical sense of turning left or right.

This experience with the actors was in line with Oliver Sacks's work with the musician Clive Wearing, whose hippocampus had been damaged by encephalitis some twenty years earlier. Wearing's memory lasted just seven seconds but he was still able to conduct, play the piano and sing complex musical works. When asked about a piece of music he seemed to remember nothing but when his hands were on the piano he could play perfectly. Similarly, there are cases of actors suffering from Alzheimer's who can still act out lengthy roles.

Increasingly scientist believe that memory is a physical and emotional response. One of the key elements in most memory techniques is forging a connection to create an emotional response or link with the material you are trying to learn.

A 2006 study by Helga and Tony Noice published in the Journal of the Association for Psychological Science comes to the same conclusions. Helga Noice is a cognitive psychologist at Elmhurst College and Tony Noice a cognitive researcher, actor and director at Indiana State University and they spent two decades making a psychological study of actors.

They found the secret of actors' abilities to learn lines is basically acting. Put more simply, when learning, actors really concentrate on the meaning of lines, their physical and emotional aspects, all the time considering ways to communicate meaning to others.

Crucially, actors break the script into a series of chunks, often called 'beats', which contain a single immediate intention as a reaction to another character. They keep asking 'why?' in order to understand a character's overall plan and intention, particularly in relation to other characters. In this way a script becomes a series of beats each logically linked with the next.

Michael Caine explains, 'You must be able to stand there not thinking of that line. You take it off the other actor's face.'

The Noices call this 'active experiencing', channelling emotions, movement and mental powers to communicate meaning. This is definitely a way of learning that can be usefully employed by non-actors. Studies have found that students who imagine explaining and conveying material to other people when they learn retain more information than those who learn by rote.

The Noices also studied the effects of their 'active

experience' principle of learning on a group of older people who took part in a four-week acting course. Afterwards the group showed significant improvements in word recall, problem-solving and memory retention with the improvements if anything more marked after a four-month gap.

Other researchers on memory have come to similar conclusions suggesting that memory relies on emotion, action and understanding.

KEY TIPS FOR LEARNING LINES

· Memorising anything takes time and you do need to make an effort.

· Really look at the words and make sure you understand.

· Say the words aloud.

· Learn lines in context. Experts emphasise 'gist' learning – understanding the meaning behind the words, the motivations and overall intentions.

· Look at the whole, then divide and subdivide right down to sentences. Really think and make sure you understand.

· One of the keys to learning is organisation and the ability to retrieve a memory.

· Break material into manageable chunks containing a single intention or idea.

· Establish logical links between each chunk or beat.

· Look for patterns. Pick out the most important words and look for the relationship between them.

· Some people favour cue or flash cards.

· Coupling information with emotions or imagining a physical action helps fix the memory.

· Retype your lines. It's amazing how much you will have retained afterwards.

· Play with what you're learning. Try handwriting a line but only write the first letter of each word.

· Tape recordings can really help, especially if you are an auditory person. They're also useful if you drive a lot as you can play them in the car. Start with your own part but then just record others' lines as a prompt for your own.

· Take time away from the material to give your brain a chance to process and store.

WEATHER

'Sunshine is delicious, rain is refreshing, wind braces up, snow is exhilarating; there is no such thing as bad weather, only different kinds of good weather'.

JOHN RUSKIN

There are many verses and sayings about the weather, most of which have become part of our folklore and seem to be assimilated rather than consciously learned. When most were composed and by whom remains unknown, but they act as general mnemonics, helping us predict and understand our weather.

RAINBOWS

The seven colours of the rainbow (or colour spectrum) have given us one of the most famous mnemonics of all:

Richard Of York Gave Battle In Vain.

Red, Orange, Yellow, Green, Blue, Indigo, Violet.

The sentence is a reference to Richard III, more particularly as portrayed in Shakespeare's eponymous play. Variations have been composed but why meddle with something that has worked well for so long?

SKIES AND RAINBOWS

Red sky at night,
Shepherds' delight.
Red sky in the morning,
Shepherds' warning.

This is one of the oldest weather sayings and sometimes includes sailors rather than shepherds which makes sense as predicting the weather is obviously very important to both.

The rhyme was probably passed on by word of mouth long before it was ever written down, but to give an indication of how ancient it is, in the New Testament, Matthew 16, verses 2 and 3 say, 'When it is evening, you say, "It will be fair, for the sky is red." And in the morning, "It will be stormy today, for the sky is red and threatening." You know how to interpret the appearance of the sky . . .'

The saying is also referenced in Shakespeare, in a line from *Venus* and *Adonis* published in 1593: 'Like a red morn that ever yet betoken'd wreck to the seaman – sorrow to shepherds.'

It does make meteorological sense. Sunlight travels through more atmosphere when it is low in the sky, at dawn and dusk. The red/orange part of the spectrum of light keeps a more direct course and is better reflected back from clouds. If there is broken cloud in the morning approaching from the west and possibly bringing rain, we are more likely to see red light reflecting back from the cloud. Red clouds at dusk suggest any storm clouds have passed giving a good chance of clear skies ahead.

> *Rainbow in the morning,*
> *Travellers take warning.*
> *Rainbow at night,*
> *Travellers' delight.*

This also has a logical explanation. Rainbows indicate humid air and as a morning rainbow would be seen in the west, the direction from which storms generally come in the United Kingdom as the wind is primarily westerly, they often appear before bad weather. On the other hand, evening rainbows which appear in the east often indicate the passing of stormy weather.

> *Morning red, evening grey,*
> *Two sure signs of one fine day.*

GOOD AND BAD WEATHER

Low pressure forces smoke down:

> *When smoke descends, good weather ends.*

> *When smoke hovers close to the ground,*
> *There will be a weather change.*

> *When down the chimney falls the soot*
> *Mud will soon be underfoot.*

In fine weather, sound waves travel upwards and outwards in

the atmosphere whereas on humid, cloudy days they are sent back to the ground:

> Sound travelling far and wide
> A stormy day this doth betide.

And along the same lines:

> When forests murmur and mountains roar,
> Close your windows and shut the door.

> When ditch and pond offend the nose,
> Look out for rain and stormy blows.

Just as sound travels farther as storms approach, so do smells.

In the northern hemisphere you can find the centre of a weather system:

> When the wind is at your back, the low is on your left.

This would be reversed in the southern hemisphere.

Pilots use the following mnemonic:

> High to Low:
> Look out below.
> Low to High:
> Clear Blue sky.

This is because if pressure temperature drops, you will be lower in altitude than the aircraft's instruments suggest if they are left uncorrected. Alternatively, a rise in pressure temperature will result in the opposite effect:

When larks fly high, expect fair weather.

From the West Country:

In March and April there be showers,
They go on for hours and hours.
Then comes May, the farmers say,
Frost by night and hail by day.
Then comes June, the sun is hot,
Is it shining? No it's not.

When March roars in like a lion, it will go out like a lamb.

Seagull, seagull, sit on the sand,
It's never good weather while you're on the land.

When seagulls fly to land,
A storm is at hand.

When the wind is in the East,
'Tis neither good for man nor beast.

TEMPERATURE

Crickets chirp faster as the temperature rises.

Cold is the night,
When stars shine bright.

And,

Clear nights, cold days.

As the days begin to shorten,
The heat begins to scorch 'em;
As the days begin to lengthen,
The cold begins to strengthen.

This should be generally true as the hottest of the summer weather and coldest winter weather tend to be after the solstices.

RAIN, RAIN, GO AWAY

Rain before seven, fine before eleven.

The louder the frog, the more rain.

When geese are cackling, here comes rain.

When grass is dry in the morning light,
Look for rain before the night.
When dew is in the grass,
Rain will never come to pass.

This does make sense in that dew forming overnight is a sign of good weather and a cloudless, clear sky, whereas the absence of dew indicates either that it is cloudy or there is a strong breeze, both of which could mean rain.

A wind from the south has rain in its mouth.

If the cows are lying down, rain is on its way.

St Swithun's Day, if it does rain
Full forty days it will remain;
St Swithun's Day, if it be fair
For forty days, 'twill rain no more.

St Swithun's Day falls on 15 July, and although probably dating from the Middle Ages, this rhyme has no basis in fact.

A summer fog for fair,
Winter fog for rain.

Ground fog in summer is usually a sign it's going to be hot and sunny later, whereas winter fog often brings rain.

If a circle forms around the moon,
It's sure to rain, very soon.

Or,

A ring around the sun or moon,
Means rain or snow coming soon.

Circles around the sun or moon are called haloes and they are formed by light refracting, or bending, as it passes through the ice crystals that form in high-level cirrus and cirrostratus clouds. Although these clouds do not themselves produce rain or snow, they often indicate an advancing low pressure system which may do so.

When leaves show their undersides,
Be very sure that rain betides.

When clouds appear like rocks and towers,
The earth's refreshed by frequent showers.

MUSIC

'After silence, that which comes closest to
expressing the inexpressible is music'.

ALDOUS HUXLEY

M nemonics play an important part in the early lessons of everyone who has ever learned to read music or play an instrument.

READING THE NOTES

The notes represented by the five lines on the treble stave from bottom to top are: E, G, B, D, F.

Every Good Boy Deserves Favours, or
Every Good Boy Deserves Fun.

The corresponding spaces in the treble clef are F, A, C, E, which spell the easily remembered, 'Face'. Or you may prefer:

Fat Angels Crash Easily.

The order of notes on the lines of the bass clef are G, B, D, F, A.

Green Birds Do Fly Away, or linking with the treble clef,

Good Boys Do Fine, Always, and the version my piano teacher taught me:

Great British Dancers Float Away.

The corresponding spaces of the bass clef are: A, C, E, G.

All Cows Eat Grass.

The order for adding sharps is called the circle of fifths: F, C, G, D, A, E, B.

Father Christmas Gets Drunk After Every Beer.
Five Cool Guys Danced Away Every Beat.
Father Charles Goes Down And Ends Battle.

This last mnemonic can be neatly reversed for the order of flats in flat key signatures, B, E, A, D, G, F, C:

Battle Ends And Down Goes Father Charles.

MUSICAL MODES

The order of musical modes

The musical modes as based on the white keys of a piano starting with middle C are: Ionian mode, Dorian mode, Phrygian mode, Lydian mode, Mixolydian mode, Aeolian mode, Locrian mode:

I Don't Punch Like Muhammad Al Lee.

GUITAR STRINGS

The strings on a standard tuned guitar beginning with the lowest, heaviest gauge string are: E, A, D, G, B, E:

Even After Dinner, Growing Boys Eat, or,
Elephants And Donkeys Grow Big Ears.

Or in the reverse order, E, B, G, D, A, E:

Excited Bunnies Get Drunk At Easter.

 SPORT

'Sports do not build character. They reveal it.'

HEYWOOD BROWN

Surprisingly, there seem to be very few mnemonics especially for sport. It may be because football results or cricket scores are something supporters feel so passionately about that they don't need mnemonics to help them remember the details. All the key elements necessary for good recall are already there – interest, intense emotion, vivid imagery and associations alongside ample opportunity for repetition while talking over the match.

FOOTBALL

Football fans may not need much help remembering crucial scores but lists of results lend themselves to the application of Pegword memory techniques and particularly the more advanced Major system (see pages 90-93). Many memory experts, including Derren Brown, successfully remember results and teams this way.

Taking World Cup winners from 1930, when the tournament began, gives ample opportunity to practise the technique.

World Cup Winners

Year	Final Teams	Score
1930	Uruguay beat Argentina	4 − 2
1934	Italy beat Czechoslovakia	2 − 1
1938	Italy beat Hungary	4 − 2
1950	Uruguay beat Brazil	2 − 1
1954	W. Germany beat Hungary	3 − 2
1958	Brazil beat Sweden	5 − 2
1962	Brazil beat Czechoslovakia	3 − 1
1966	England beat W. Germany	4 − 2
1970	Brazil beat Italy	4 − 1
1974	W. Germany beat Holland	2 − 1
1978	Argentina beat Holland	3 − 1
1982	Italy beat W. Germany	3 − 1
1986	Argentina beat W. Germany	3 − 2
1990	Germany beat Argentina	1 − 0
1994	Brazil beat Italy (on penalties)	3 − 2
1998	France beat Brazil	3 − 0
2002	Brazil beat Germany	2 − 0
2006	Italy beat France (on penalties)	5 − 3

Applying the Major system to the most recent final, split the year 2006 into 20 − n and s/z which suggests the word 'nose'; and 06 − s/z and j/g, sh or ch; trickier but it could make 'sash', creating an image to represent the year of a nose wrapped in a scarlet sash announcing nose of the year.

Next the teams and scores. These are most simply reduced to I-5 and F-3, which then make I-l and F-m and could translate to 'ill' or 'hill' and 'farm'. The image to remember the whole thing then becomes a farmer with a large, scarlet-sash-wrapped nose (2006) surveying his farm (France 3) perched precariously on top of a hill (Italy 5).

As another example, taking the 19 for granted, '86 becomes f-sh or 'fish', and the teams and scores, Argentina – A-3 or A-m to give 'arm', and W. Germany – WG-2 or WG-n suggesting 'wagon'. So the image would become: a fish ('86) driving a wagon (W. Germany 2) of arms (Argentina 3) – these could be either weapons or literally severed arms which is probably a more bizarre and therefore memorable picture.

The success of applying the mnemonic technique obviously depends on your being completely familiar with the 'pegs' and you should choose the words and images that seem most obvious and appealing to you. The very effort of thinking so hard about each result should help to lodge it firmly in your brain.

CRICKET

There are ten Test Cricket nations: Australia, Bangladesh, England India, New Zealand, Pakistan, South Africa, Sri Lanka, West Indies and Zimbabwe.

These two sentences should help prompt your memory for them all:

A Bad Egg Is Never Pleasant. So Stroke Wild Zebras.

DRESSAGE

A simple way to memorise the location of the letters in a dressage ring is to remember the sentence:

All King Edward's Horses Can Mount Big Fences eXceptionally.

Which is easier than:

A, K, E, H, C, M, B, F, X.

These are the basics. At higher levels the letters are, A, K, V, E, S, H, C, M, R, B, P, F.
Remember them as:

All King Victor's Exceptional Show Horses Can Mount Regal Barriers Placed Fantastically.

Finally, the centre line, D, L, X, I, G, can be recalled by:

David Licks eXciting Ice Granitas.

```
        Dressage arena
        K  V  E  S  H
Enter A D  L  X  I  G   C
        F  P  B  R  M
```

SAILING

Tying a bowline

The most commonly used mnemonic to remind yourself how to tie a bowline involves a rabbit, or occasionally a fox. Either would work:

> *The rabbit pops up out of his hole, hops around the tree*
> *and disappears back down into the hole again.*

Translated, the 'hole' is a small loop in the standing line leading to the fixed object. Hold the small loop in your hand and pass the free end behind your back (the tree). The rabbit is the free end of the rope and this comes up out of the loop, passes around the standing line (the tree) and goes back down through the loop. To complete the knot, tighten so that it looks something like a seat. The resulting large loop will not tighten when it is lifted.

I am told this is also very useful for a climbing harness. The following rhyme is supposed to clarify the details:

> *Lay the bight to make a hole*
> *Then under the back and around the pole.*
> *Over the top and through the eye*
> *Cinch it tight and let it lie.*

I am not sure that it helps very much without a clear diagram or, better still, someone demonstrating.

Navigation

To make sure you don't hit the shore when entering a harbour it's worth remembering the simple line for which side the red light should be on:

Red on right upon return.

SETTING UP A SNOOKER TABLE

The coloured balls are placed on the D from left to right in order: Green, Brown, Yellow, which can be remembered as

God Bless You.

GAMES

The Order of Suits in Bridge

Spades,
Hearts,
Diamonds,
Clubs.

Just think:

Sally Has Dirty Children.

CHURCHILL'S MEMORY

Everyone remembers Churchill as a great orator, never at a loss for words, and with a wealth of quotations from poetry and literature at his disposal. But what many do not realise is that this did not come naturally; it took him years of practice and hard work.

As a boy, Winston Churchill suffered from a speech impediment and yet in his first year at Harrow School, he won a contest reciting 1,300 lines of poetry from memory. He liked words and was determined; he simply persevered until he overcame the impediment.

During World War II, he wrote and delivered speeches that defined key moments in British and world history. Again he studied and practised.

His private secretary, John Colville, calculated that Churchill devoted one hour of preparation for every minute of delivery time. He also used every moment. There are stories of him shaving with poems attached to the bathroom mirror so that even those few minutes every day could be purposeful.

CLASSICS
AND MYTHOLOGY

*'[Memory is] a man's real possession . . .
In nothing else is he rich, in nothing else
is he poor.'*

This section somehow conjures up images of Molesworth and classrooms of pupils chanting Latin verbs. I've omitted those but instead included just a few examples which interested me.

GREAT PHILOSOPHERS

To remember who came first, or who was influenced by whom, just think of the word:

SPA

Socrates 469 – 399 BC Renowned for his contribution to ethics, credited as one of the founders of western philosophy although he wrote nothing down.

Plato 428 – 348 BC His *Dialogues* are the most comprehensive account of Socrates that we have. His writings have been used to teach a range of subjects including, philosophy, logic, rhetoric and maths.

Aristotle 384 – 322 BC A student of Plato and teacher of Alexander the Great.

Plato, together with his mentor, Socrates, and pupil, Aristotle, helped to lay the foundations of Western and natural philosophy, ethics, and science.

ROMAN NUMERALS

1	5	10	50	100	500	1000
I	V	X	L	C	D	M

These sentences help you remember them in order:

I Veered across, Lucy Can't Drink Milk, and
I Value Xylophones Like Cows Dig Milk.

THE SEVEN HILLS OF ROME

The hills are called:

Caelian, Quirinal, Viminal, Esquiline, Capitoline, Aventine, Palatine.

These can be remembered by the question:

Can Queen Victoria Eat Cold Apple Pie?

The seven hills form the geographical heart of Rome within the ancient city walls. The city was said to have been founded by Romulus on the Palatine Hill.

The emperors' palaces were built on the Palatine Hill, which is where the word palace comes from. If Nero really did burn Rome in AD 64 when four-fifths of the city was destroyed, he would have watched the blaze from the Palatine Hill. The ruined courts of the Flavian Palace, together with some mosaic paving and sculptures in the Palatine Museum, are all that remain today.

THE THREE GRACES

The Graces were the goddess daughters of Jupiter in Roman mythology and of Zeus in Greek. They were known in Latin as the Gratiae and in ancient Greek as the Charities. They represent Charm, Beauty and Creativity and have inspired countless sculptors and painters, famously the sixteenth-century painting by Raphael and nineteenth-century sculpture by Canova.

Their names are Euphrosyne, Aglaia and Thalmia, prompted by:

EAT, or

You-frostily Agreed Terms.

To remember that they symbolise creativity, beauty and charm, think of:

CBC, or *Create Beautiful Children*.

THE MUSES

The Muses are the goddesses or spirits who are said to inspire the creation of literature and the arts. At first there were said to be three in Classical Greece but by 400 BC their number had grown to nine.

There are various stories about their origins but, most appropriately for a book about memory, Hesiod's *Theogeny*, written in the seventh century BC, claims they were the daughters of Zeus and Mnemosyne, the goddess of memory.

Their names are:

Muse	*Most associated with*	*Symbol*
Calliope	Epic poetry	Writing tablet
Euterpe	Music	Flute
Clio	History	Scroll
Terpsichore	Dance	Lyre
Thalia	Comedy	Comic mask
Urania	Astronomy	Globe and compass
Polyhymnia	Choral poetry	Veil
Melpomene	Tragedy	Tragic mask
Erato	Lyric poetry	7-stringed lyre or guitar

This mnemonic sentence helps to prompt their names:

Calling Every Classics Teacher That Understands Pollyanna's Mental Error.

SCIENTIFIC SURPRISES

• In April 2007, scientists at Columbia University found that it may be possible for people to have 'too much memory'. This makes it harder for them to filter out and assimilate information, increasing the time it takes for new short-term memories to be processed and stored.

• University of Adelaide researchers found the time of day at which students study influences their ability to learn. Surprisingly, it seems that our brains learn more effectively in the evening.

• This may be because sleep tends to follow evening study sessions and increasing evidence suggests the brain needs sleep to record information, playing it back to itself as we slumber.

• Age isn't always a disadvantage when it comes to memory. A Nature Neuroscience report shows adults can outperform children in remembering the contextual, more complex details.

MEMORY GAMES

'The memory should be specially taxed in youth, since it is then that it is strongest and most tenacious. But in choosing the things that should be committed to memory the utmost care and forethought must be exercised; as lessons well learnt in youth are never forgotten.'

ARTHUR SCHOPENHAUER

Some of my best memories of primary school are from break time and many of the games we played obsessively again and again are in essence memory games. Here are just a few.

THE CONCENTRATION GAME

As with many good games it starts with everyone sitting in a circle. Each person has a number which they must remember. First the rhythm is set. Everyone slaps their knees twice then claps their hands twice. This is repeated a few times so that everyone is together then one person chants:

'Are you ready?' slap slap clap clap. 'Are you sure?' slap slap clap clap. 'Let's begin,' slap slap clap clap.

The person who is number one answers, 'One one,' followed by someone else's number chosen at random. So it could go, 'One one seven seven,' slap slap clap clap.'

Then person number seven answers adding another person's number without breaking the rhythm, 'Seven seven two two,' slap slap clap clap.

If anyone falters, forgets their number or breaks the rhythm they are out.

KIM'S GAME

Named after Kipling's eponymous hero, this was always popular at birthday parties and I particularly liked it because it didn't require any physical effort or skill from me, just an attention to detail. The more you play, the better you get. By the end of the party season there was usually serious competition.

The setup is simple: all you need is a tray upon which a variety of small objects are arranged; between ten and twenty is probably ideal. The player is asked to study the tray carefully for a moment or so, then turns away while one of the objects is taken away. The trick is to remember and identify what's missing. There are variations where more than one object is taken or the tray is rearranged. You can even bluff by not removing anything.

THE TRAY GAME

I think this variation of Kim's game is less fun but its advantage is that it can be played by several people at the same time. The tray is again set up with ten to twenty small items which everyone studies for a moment. The tray is then covered over and everyone is asked to write down each item they remember as quickly as possible. It's best to set a time limit and the winner is the person who remembers the most objects the fastest.

PARACHUTE GAME

Everyone forms a circle and carefully looks around to memorise who is there. One person is chosen to go outside and while they are gone, another person hides beneath the parachute (or blanket). When the person returns, they must guess who is hiding. This works well when children are first getting to know one another, in the early days of a new school year or club, but it can also work as a party game.

MIXED MEMORY

As a variation of one person hiding, two people can also switch places and the person returning to the room must work out who. Or instead of people switching, furniture or objects can be moved.

EYEWITNESS REPORTS

Act out a scene or show a clip to a group. Afterwards, ask everyone to write down exactly what they saw, together with details of clothing, what was said, how long everything took. Compare accounts to find out just how reliable eyewitnesses really are.

PICNIC BASKET

This game can take many forms. Sometimes it begins with, 'I'm going on a picnic and in my basket I have strawberries . . .' the next person continues with 'I'm going on a picnic and in my basket I have strawberries and cream.' The third person remembers both previous ingredients and adds another of their choosing and so on. The object of the game is to remember each item on the list adding another when it's your turn. People are out if they forget something and the winner is the last person to make a mistake.

The game can also start with 'I'm going to the super-market to buy . . .' or 'I'm going to visit Grandma and in my bag I have . . .' Items on the list can be themed or as quirky and miscellaneous as you please. If you're keen on winning, it's a good idea to choose something quite dull and forgettable when it's your turn.

FINAL
THOUGHTS

'Our memory is like a shop in the window of which is exposed now one, now another photograph of the same person. And as a rule the most recent exhibit remains for some time the only one to be seen'.

MARCEL PROUST

I hope that after reading this book it is not only the most recent entries to your memory store that can be readily accessed. If nothing else, the collection of mnemonics is intended to remind you of things you once knew but had mislaid in the recesses of your memory and introduced others that you perhaps never knew but which you find interesting. Above all, I hope it's made you realise that learning things can be fun; that few people have perfect memories but that we can all remember better. It should have helped highlight your strengths and weaknesses and what works best for you.

There are no real quick fixes. Committing anything to memory always involves some effort, but with the right approach any work involved should bring satisfying results and be enjoyable.

'The secret of a good memory is attention, and attention to a subject depends upon our interest in it. We rarely forget that which has made a deep impression on our minds.'

TRYON EDWARDS

ACKNOWLEDGEMENTS

First and foremost I should like to thank all those nameless individuals and groups who originally came up with the many varied mnemonic lines and verses included here. There are also a range of websites and books which have proved invaluable for research, particularly: eudesign.com, mindtools.com, OxfordOnline.com, quotationspage.com, the *Oxford Dictionary of Quotations* and *Brewer's Dictionary of Phrase and Fable*.

On a personal note, thank you to the publisher who originally suggested the idea for the book and to Jo Caseby for her clear thinking and encouragement just when it was most needed. Also to so many friends and family for their contributions, and to Nicola Taplin and the team at Preface.

While every effort has been made to contact copyright holders, the author and publisher would be grateful for information about any material where they have been unable to trace the source, and would be glad to make amendments in further editions.